COME, LET US
PRAISE HIM

covenant press

ISBN 910452-57-1
Copyright © 1985 by Covenant Press

covenant press

3200 West Foster Avenue   Chicago, Illinois 60625

800-621-1290   312-478-4676

FOREWORD

Covenant history literally resonates with the splendor of music and song. Emerging as it did from the deeper meanings of new life in Jesus Christ, it is filled with praise, adoration, and gladness of heart.

To attempt to celebrate the Covenant's Centennial without special attention to its rich heritage of hymnody would be to misrepresent both the tone and the spirit of our beginnings and life. Hence this compilation, superbly prepared by the Commission on Church Music and Worship, replete with hymns of heritage and gospel songs both contemporary and traditional. Included also is the Centennial hymn for the Covenant.

Praise is comely to the Christian and it is never done better than with the beauty, dignity, and grandeur of singing. So let us with joy and gladness join together and hail the publication of this Centennial hymnal by using it to sing praise to God.

Milton B. Engebretson, president
The Evangelical Covenant Church

PREFACE

Come, Let Us Praise Him was prepared especially for the Centennial
celebration of the Evangelical Covenant Church. Although many of the
songs are favorites from *The Covenant Hymnal* (1973), at least one
third are from other sources, thus making this a potential supplement to
our present songbook. A number of hymns are taken from *The
Covenant Hymnal* (1935), and two later collections of songs for trial use
in the churches, *New Hymns and Translations*, Nos. 1 and 2 (1978,
1981). Also included are the prize-winning Centennial hymn and two
others of recent composition.

Because the collection is not intended as a complete hymn-book, the
songs are not arranged in any specific order. However, they are divided
into four different categories: *Heritage, Classic/Traditional, Gospel,*
and *Contemporary.* There is also an index of titles and first lines.

The volume has been compiled by the Covenant Commission on
Church Music and Worship and produced by Covenant Press. Members
of the commission are: Vernon Anderson, Jonathan Brown, A. Royce
Eckhardt, J. Irving Erickson, James R. Hawkinson, Jonathan Larson,
and William MacPherson. Every effort has been made to trace the
ownership of all copyrights. If any omissions have occurred, subsequent
editions will be corrected on notification by copyright holders.

It is the Commission's prayer that *Come, Let Us Praise Him* will find
joyful and extensive use, not only during the Centennial but in years to
come as we unite in the worship and service of God.

J. Irving Erickson, chairman
Commission on Church Music and Worship

James R. Hawkinson
Executive Secretary of Covenant Publications

CONTENTS

Heritage Hymns   1-30

Classic/Traditional   31-57

Gospel Hymns   58-83

Contemporary   84-100

Index

Heritage Hymns

Praise the Lord, All Praise and Blessing 1

Joel Blomqvist, 1840-1930
Tr. Gerhard W. Palmgren, 1880-1959

LOVEN HERREN 8.7.8.7.7.7.
Joel Blomqvist, 1840-1930

1 Praise the Lord, all praise and bless - ing Ren - der to his might - y name; Thank him ev - er for his good-ness, Now and ev - er - more the same. Come, my soul, your trib - ute bring, Praise him ev - 'ry liv - ing thing.

2 He cre - at - ed earth and heav - en, Deep - est sea and all there - in; Small-est crea - ture, high - est be - ing, Let your an - thems now be - gin. Bless him in this glad - some hour, Bless his maj - es - ty and pow'r.

3 Stars a - bove in bril - liant glo - ry, Sun that scat - ters wide its gold, Birds a - loft, all join the cho - rus, Ev - 'ry crea - ture, young and old, Sing to him who reigns su - preme, Chant that ev - er - joy - ful theme.

4 Yet of all that God cre - at - ed Hu - man - kind most pre - cious is; O what won - der - ful de - vo - tion, How it fills my heart with bliss! With a child - like joy I sing Prais - es to my God and King!

5 God so loved this world of sin - ners That his on - ly Son he gave To en - dure death's bit - ter an - guish And the lost to seek and save. Let our prais - es rend the sky, Glo - ry be to God on high. A - men.

2 O Mighty God, When I Behold the Wonder

Carl Boberg, 1859-1940
Tr. E. Gustav Johnson, 1893-1974

O STORE GUD 11.10.11.10. *with Refrain*
Swedish Folk Melody
Harm. by Norman E. Johnson, 1928-1983

1 O might-y God, when I be-hold the won-der
2 When I be - hold the heav-ens in their vast - ness,
3 When I hear fools in ig - nor-ance and fol - ly
4 When crushed by guilt of sin, be - fore thee kneel - ing
5 And when at last the mists of time have van - ished

Of na - ture's beau - ty, wrought by words of thine,
Where gold - en ships in az - ure is - sue forth,
De - ny thee, God, and taunt thy ho - ly word,
I plead for mer - cy and for grace and peace,
And I in truth my faith con - firmed shall see,

And how thou lead - est all from realms up - yon - der,
Where sun and moon keep watch up - on the fast - ness
And yet per - ceive that thou sup - pli - eth whol - ly
I feel thy balm and, all my bruis - es heal - ing,
Up - on the shores where earth - ly ills are ban - ished

Sus - tain - ing earth - ly life with love be - nign,
Of chang-ing sea - sons and of time on earth,
Their ev - 'ry need, thy love in grace con - ferred,
My soul is filled, my heart is set at ease.
I'll en - ter, Lord, to dwell in peace with thee.

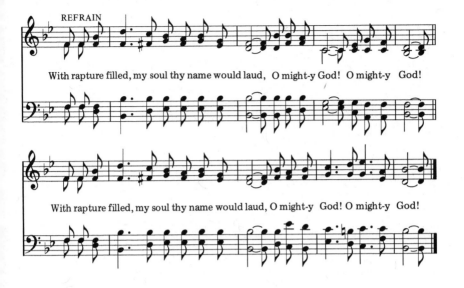

REFRAIN

With rapture filled, my soul thy name would laud, O might-y God! O might-y God!

With rapture filled, my soul thy name would laud, O might-y God! O might-y God!

Be filled with the Spirit; addressing one another in psalms and hymns and spiritual songs, singing and making melody to the Lord with all your heart.

Ephesians 5:18,19

Singing was prominent in these services. The whole congregation would join in the unaffected and beautiful songs which were willingly led by brothers and sisters who had the gift. At the conclusion of the sermon it seemed as if the singing would not end. A verse, or perhaps only a refrain, would be repeated again and again until the words were impressed upon our minds and "joy stood high in the ceiling!"

C.M. Youngquist, *Hem-Missionären,*
Tr. Eric G. Hawkinson, *Images in Covenant Beginnings*

3 Our Mighty God Works Mighty Wonders

Nils Frykman, 1842-1911
Tr. A. L. Skoog, 1856-1934
Tr. Andrew T. Frykman, 1875-1943

CELEBRATION 9.8.9.8.8.8.
Swedish Folk Melody

1 Our might-y God works might-y won-ders— What joy to
2 His might-y word goes forth to con-quer, Its pow'r de-
3 Be-hold the faith-ful host is near-ing The gates of
4 Dear Lord, as throngs thy king-dom en-ter, May not my
5 O God be praised! the day is near-ing, When to our

see them all a-round! All i-dols fall be-fore his thun-ders,
stroys the forts of doubt; The war-riors bold yield up their ar-mor
heav'n with might-y tread; With ban-ners wav-ing, sing-ing, cheer-ing,
heart thy love de-cline; Teach me my faith on thee to cen-ter,
ears a voice shall come, "Look up! the Lord is now ap-pear-ing,

Their al-tars crum-bling to the ground. He breaks the
To him who will not cast them out. They cleans-ing
They hail in joy their roy-al Head; And man-y
Thy grace shall make me whol-ly thine. Take thou my
To gath-er all his loved ones home!" O bless-ed

fet-ters, frees the slaves, His fall-en chil-dren still he saves.
find in Je-sus' blood And laud and mag-ni-fy our God.
more shall own his reign, His won-drous love the vic-t'ry gain.
hand and hold it fast, Un-til I reach thy heav'n at last.
day of ju-bi-lee! For thee I wait! I wait for thee!

Praise the Lord with Joyful Song

A. L. Skoog, 1856-1934
Tr. E. Gustav Johnson, 1893-1974

LOVEN GUD 7.6.7.6. with Refrain
A. L. Skoog, 1856-1934

4

1 Praise the Lord with joy - ful song, U - nite with full ac - cord!
2 Praise him for his maj - es - ty, His great and glo - rious pow'r!
3 Praise him with the sound of harps, With mu - sic loud and clear!
4 Praise him with har - mo - nious chimes, With chords of joy pro - claim!

For his glo - ry and his might Sing prais - es to the Lord!
Hail him with a wor - thy hymn, Ex - alt his name this hour!
With glad strains of mel - o - dy Our gra - cious God re - vere!
Great and ho - ly is the Lord: Sing prais - es to his name!

REFRAIN

Sing his prais-es, ev-'ry liv - ing thing, Un - to him de-vo-ted hom-age bring,

Of his love and good-ness ev - er sing! Hal - le - lu - jah! Praise the Lord!

5   How Great the Joy the Lord Provides

Nils Frykman, 1842-1911
Tr. Aaron Markuson, 1910-
Tr. Glen V. Wiberg, 1925-

DAY OF REDEMPTION 8.6.8.6.8.8. *with Refrain*
"Engelke's Lofsånger," 1871

1 How great the joy the Lord pro-vides For us so free-ly here, When at his ta-ble he pre-sides And we to him draw near! His grace is new each day and hour, And we can rest up-on his pow'r.

2 It is so good to love the Lord, Who gave his life for all. So good to trust his liv-ing Word, Be lift-ed when we fall. When earth-ly plea-sures reach their end, Our feast of joy will just be-gin.

3 When shad-ows come, as come they will, And gloom per-vades the day, When hopes once bright grow cold and chill, The Lord pro-vides a way. In heav'n his light will al-ways shine, And bless-ed-ness be yours and mine. Hal-

4 So let us not be filled with care For home and dai-ly bread. In grace the Lord his love will share And sure-ly we'll be fed. Through all our days he's by our side, He bears what-ev-er may be-tide.

5 With joy we walk with Je-sus here, How great a friend is he! But think what joy a-waits us there, When heav-en's light we see. Our hopes and dreams will be com-plete, When at the heav'n-ly feast we meet.

REFRAIN

Words copyright 1978 by Covenant Press.

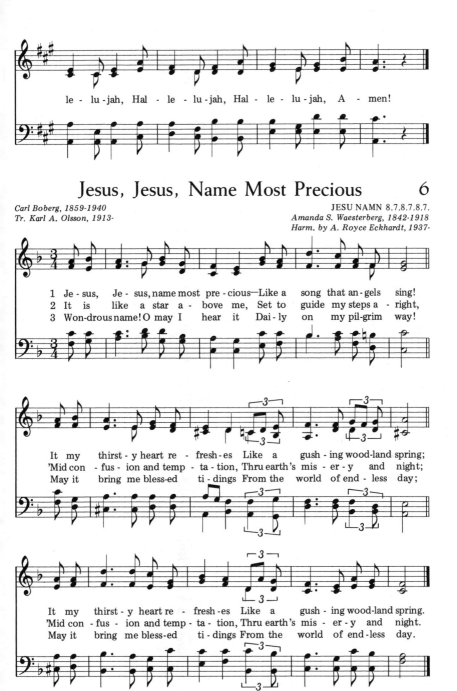

le - lu -jah, Hal - le - lu -jah, Hal - le - lu -jah, A - men!

Jesus, Jesus, Name Most Precious 6

Carl Boberg, 1859-1940
Tr. Karl A. Olsson, 1913-

JESU NAMN 8.7.8.7.8.7.
Amanda S. Waesterberg, 1842-1918
Harm. by A. Royce Eckhardt, 1937-

1 Je - sus, Je - sus, name most pre - cious—Like a song that an - gels sing!
2 It is like a star a - bove me, Set to guide my steps a - right,
3 Won-drous name! O may I hear it Dai - ly on my pil-grim way!

It my thirst - y heart re - fresh-es Like a gush - ing wood-land spring;
'Mid con - fus - ion and temp - ta - tion, Thru earth's mis - er - y and night;
May it bring me bless-ed ti - dings From the world of end - less day;

It my thirst - y heart re - fresh-es Like a gush - ing wood-land spring.
'Mid con - fus - ion and temp - ta - tion, Thru earth's mis - er - y and night.
May it bring me bless-ed ti - dings From the world of end-less day.

7   Chosen Seed and Zion's Children

Anders Carl Rutström, 1721-1772
Tr. Claude W. Foss, 1855-1935

LAMMETS FOLK 8.7.8.7.D.
Attr. to Anders Carl Rutström, 1721-1772
"Sions Nya Sånger," 1854

1 Cho - sen seed and Zi - on's chil - dren, Ran - somed from e -
2 Still re - joice a - mid thy tri - als, Nor re - gard thy
3 Pleas- ant - ly thy lines have fall - en Un - der - neath the
4 Faith and love are the con - di - tions— All on faith and
5 And up - on this blest foun - da - tion, Lord, our Lord and

ter - nal wrath, Trav - 'ling to the heav'n - ly Ca - naan
lot a - miss, For the kind and lov - ing Sav - ior
tree of life, For the Lord is thy sal - va - tion
love de - pends; Love of law is the ful - fill - ment,
Sav - ior - King, May thy Spir - it e'er u - nite us,

On a rough and thorn - y path: Church of God, in
Is the source of all thy bliss. May he ev - er
And thy shield in all thy strife. Here the tim - id
Faith God's mer - cy ap - pre - hends: Who hath faith shall
To it may we ev - er cling. May we, mem - bers

Christ e - lect - ed, Thou to God art rec - on - ciled; But on earth thou
be thy por - tion, He who gave thee life and breath; In his keep - ing
bird finds shel - ter, Here the swal - low finds a nest, Trem - bling fu - gi -
see sal - va - tion, Who hath love shall life ob - tain; May, O Lord, thy
of one bod - y, Grow in - to a per - fect whole; Grant, O Lord, that

Words used by permission of Fortress Press.

art   a   stran - ger,   Per - se - cut - ed   and   re - viled.
fear no   e - vil,   Now or   in   the   hour of   death.
tive   a   ref - uge,   And the wea - ry   pil - grim rest.
love pos - sess us   And thy Spir - it   in   us   reign.
in   thy peo - ple   There may be   one   heart and soul.   A - men.

In Thy Temple Courts, O Father   8

David Nyvall, 1863-1946   LAMMETS FOLK 8.7.8.7.D.
Tr. E. Gustav Johnson, 1893-1974   *Attr. to Anders Carl Rutström, 1721-1772*
                                                "Sions Nya Sånger," 1854

1   In thy temple courts, O Father, Once again assembled now,
     Sing we praises as we gather, In contrition humbly bow.
     Here a foretaste we are given Of the holy sabbath peace
     Which for us is stored in heaven, When life's woes and strife shall cease.

2   For the hour of mercy granted We present our heartfelt praise;
     Thanks, O Lord, for truths implanted, Thanks for tokens of thy grace.
     Thanks for warnings, for instruction, Thanks for new-born hope received;
     Thanks for light—blind fear's destruction, For anxiety relieved.

3   Help us now thy word to cherish, Sanctify our service, Lord!
     That thy truth our souls may nourish, Be thy will in us restored!
     Help us in our daily living, As we face the days ahead,
     That we may be always giving Room to thee, by thee be led. Amen.

Let the word of Christ dwell in you richly, teach and admonish one
another in all wisdom, and sing psalms and hymns and spiritual songs
with thankfulness in your hearts to God.

                                        Colossians 3:16

9 O Let Your Soul Now Be Filled with Gladness

Peter Jönsson Aschan, 1726-1813
Tr. Karl A. Olsson, 1913-

RANSOMED SOUL 10.8.10.8.8.10.10.8.
Swedish Folk Melody
Harm. by A. Royce Eckhardt, 1937-

1 O let your soul now be filled with glad - ness, Your heart re-deemed, re-
2 If you seem emp - ty of an - y feel - ing, Re-joice—you are his
3 It is a good ev - 'ry good tran -scend-ing That Christ has died for

joice in - deed! O may the thought ban-ish all your sad - ness That
ran-somed bride! If those you cher - ish seem not to love you, And
you and me! It is a glad - ness that has no end - ing There-

in his blood you have been freed, That God's un - fail - ing love is yours,
dark as - sails from ev - 'ry side, Still yours the prom-ise, come what may,
in God's won-drous love to see! Praise be to you, O spot-less Lamb,

That you the on - ly Son were giv - en, That by his
In loss and tri - umph, in laugh-ter, cry - ing, In want and
Who thru the des - ert my soul are lead - ing To that fair

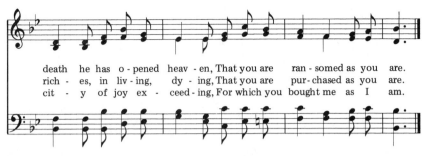

death	he has o - pened	heav - en,	That you are	ran - somed as you	are.
rich -	es, in liv - ing,	dy - ing,	That you are	pur - chased as you	are.
cit -	y of joy ex -	ceed - ing,	For which you	bought me as I	am.

Come, Let Us Praise Him 10

Lina Sandell, 1832-1903
Tr. Karl A. Olsson, 1913-

LÅTOM OSS SJUNGA 5.6.5.6.6.
Ahnfelt's "Sånger," 1868
Harm. by A. Royce Eckhardt, 1937-

1	Come, let us	praise him,	Sing-ing of grace di - vine;	Youths now and
2	Earth and the	heav -ens	Show forth his glo-ry bright;	Yet he was
3	Will - ing - ly	stoop-ing	Un - der my bur - den, he	Pa - tient-ly
4	Bear - ing our	an - guish,	Nailed to a shame-ful tree,	He died to
5	All this he	suf - fered	For his be-lov - ed bride,	That she for-
6	Let us be	sing - ing	Al - ways of him, our friend,	Ev - er a-

eld - ers	Prais - ing his love's de - sign,	Laud-ing his acts be - nign.
hum-bled,	Stripped of his won-drous might,	Shar-ing our hu - man plight.
car - ried	All that op - press-es me,	Set - ting the cap - tive free.
save us	From an e - ter - ni - ty	Of deep-est mis - er - y.
ev - er,	By his death sanc-ti - fied,	Might in his house a - bide.
dor - ing	Mer - cies with - out an end:	Christ, we our prais-es lend.

11   I Sing with Joy and Gladness

Nils Frykman, 1842-1911
Tr. E. Gustav Johnson, 1893-1974

JOYFUL PILGRIM 13.13.13.8.
Nils Frykman, 1842-1911

1 I sing with joy and glad - ness, my soul has found re - lease;
2 My for - mer res - o - lu - tions to lead a bet - ter life
3 When thoughts of guilt op - press me and I thru weak - ness fail,
4 The e - vil ad - ver - sar - y may in his fu - ry smite;
5 Thus march - ing on cou - ra - geous, with joy I see my goal —

Now free from sin and sad - ness, with God I live in peace:
Were on - ly vain il - lu - sions — my soul was still at strife:
The Sav - ior yet will bless me, his mer - cy does pre - vail:
I fear not, for I car - ry God's ar - mor in the fight:
The bless - ing of the a - ges, the ha - ven of my soul:

His ev - er - last - ing mer - cy to me has been re -
Now on the love of Je - sus com - plete - ly I re -
For - give - ness for the sin - ner his lov - ing heart pro -
The word, di - vine and might - y, shall vic - to - ry ob -
And on the pil - grim jour - ney my voice in song I

vealed, His truth in my heart has been sealed.
ly — For me he was will - ing to die.
vides, His faith - ful - ness ev - er a - bides.
tain, Its strength shall for - ev - er re - main.
raise, My God and my Sav - ior to praise.

My God, When I Consider

Nils Frykman, 1842-1911
Tr. Signe L. Bennett, 1900-
Tr. Glen V. Wiberg, 1925-

12

MARVEL 7.6.7.6.D.
From "Hemlandsånger," 1877

1 My God, when I con - si - der What you have done for me, The
2 Thru ag - o - ny and suf - f'ring You bore my ev - 'ry sin, And
3 How blest to have this treas - ure As fore-taste of my home, The
4 Why should I then be griev - ing When hav - ing such a friend? No,

grace you dai - ly of - fer That I in won - der see. My
o - ver me kept watch - ing My wan-d'ring heart to win. Would
joy that knows no mea - sure Is mine in God a - lone. His
rath - er I'd be sing - ing Un - til my jour-ney's end. So

heart is filled with rap - ture, With joy your name I laud, All
life be worth the liv - ing, What fu - ture could I know, If
lov - ing hand pro - tects me, His grace—each morn-ing new; 'Mid
I will sound his prais - es Of faith - ful - ness and grace, I'll

praise my heav'n-ly Fa - ther, All praise dear Lamb of God.
I were not for - giv - en, And grace were not be - stowed?
per - ils of the jour - ney I find his prom-ise true.
sing through end-less ag - es Be - yond all time and space.

13 Thanks to God for My Redeemer

August Ludvig Storm, 1862-1914
Tr. Carl E. Backstrom, 1901-1984

TACK O GUD 8.7.8.7.D.
J. A. Hultman, 1861-1942

1 Thanks to God for my Re - deem- er, Thanks for all thou dost pro - vide!
2 Thanks for prayers that thou hast answered Thanks for what thou dost de - ny!
3 Thanks for ros - es by the way-side, Thanks for thorns their stems contain!

Thanks for times now but a mem-'ry, Thanks for Je - sus by my side!
Thanks for storms that I have weath-ered, Thanks for all thou dost sup - ply!
Thanks for home and thanks for fire - side, Thanks for hope, that sweet re-frain!

Thanks for pleas - ant, balm-y spring-time, Thanks for dark and drear-y fall!
Thanks for pain and thanks for pleas- ure, Thanks for com-fort in de - spair!
Thanks for joy and thanks for sor - row, Thanks for heav'n-ly peace with thee!

Thanks for tears by now for - got-ten, Thanks for peace with-in my soul!
Thanks for grace that none can meas-ure, Thanks for love be-yond compare!
Thanks for hope in the to - mor-row, Thanks thru all e - ter - ni - ty! A - men.

I Have a Friend Who Loveth Me   14

Nils Frykman, 1842-1911

FRYKMAN L.M. *with Refrain*
Nils Frykman, 1842-1911
Harm. by A. Royce Eckhardt, 1937-

1 I have a friend who lov-eth me, He gave his life on Cal-va-ry;
2 My Sav-ior's love, so full and free, Doth light the wea-ry way for me;
3 I have a friend, a might-y friend, Up-on his pow'r I may de-pend;
4 O sin-ner, join us in our song! This friend to you would fain be-long;

Up-on the cross my sins he bore, And I am saved for-ev-er-more.
It fills with joy each pass-ing day And drives my sor-rows all a-way.
He reign-eth o-ver ev-'ry land, O'er val-ley, hill, o'er sea and strand.
Tho' far from what you'd like to be, His grace suf-fi-cient is for thee.

REFRAIN

O hal-le-lu-jah, he's my friend! He guides me to the jour-ney's end;

He walks be-side me all the way And will be-stow a crown some day.

15 The Highest Joy That Can Be Known

Nils Frykman, 1842-1911
Tr. Signe L. Bennett, 1900-
Tr. Andrew T. Frykman, 1875-1943

HIGHEST JOY 8.6.8.6.8.6.
Amanda S. Waesterberg, 1842-1918

1 The high-est joy that can be known By those who
2 The Word does give me wealth un - told, All good it
3 How oft-en when in deep de - spair My soul has
4 It tells me of a love di - vine, How Je - sus'
5 When stars a - bove shall shine no more, God's Word is

heav'n - ward wend— It is the Word of Life to
has in store; My deep-est sor - rows yield their
been re - stored; And when the tempt - er would en-
blood was shed; Each day this joy - ous song is
still my light; When pleas-ures of this world are

own, And God to have as friend; It is the
hold To joys for - ev - er - more; My deep-est
snare 'Twould strength to stand af - ford; And when the
mine As paths of grace I tread; Each day this
o'er, My joys will reach their height; When pleas-ures

Word of Life to own, And God to have as friend.
sor - rows yield their hold To joys for - ev - er - more.
tempt - er would en - snare 'Twould strength to stand af - ford.
joy - ous song is mine As paths of grace I tread.
of this world are o'er, My joys will reach their height.

When My Lord Is Dear to Me

16

Nils Frykman, 1842-1911
Tr. Lennart E. Anderson, 1911-

PENNOCK 7.7.7.7. *with Refrain*
Nils Frykman, 1842-1911

1 When my Lord is   dear to me,   Joy is mine, wher - e'er I be,
2 When his peace a - bides with me,   Joy is mine e - ter - nal-ly,
3 Peace, con-tent-ment, joy are mine,   What a her - it - age di-vine!
4 Kept thru faith in   Christ a - bove,   Shel-tered in his   arms of love,

Wheth - er dark and   drear the way,   Or, like E - den, fair as day.
When the sun shines fair and bright,   When it shad - ows in - to night.
With the pearl su - preme-ly rare,   Earth - ly gold can - not com-pare.
In what-ev - er may be - fall,   He is now my   all in all!

Hal - le - lu - jah! Hal - le - lu - jah! Je - sus is my friend!

He is faith - ful to de - fend His re-deemed un - to the end.

17 I Sing of the Savior

J. A. Hultman, 1861-1942
Tr. E. Gustav Johnson, 1893-1974

O NU VILL JAG SJUNGA
11.8.11.8. *with Refrain*
J. A. Hultman, 1861-1942

1 I sing of the Sav-ior whose death made me whole, Of
2 How bliss-ful the soul who be - lieves in the Lord, Who
3 We jour-ney in joy to the man - sions of light, To -
4 The blood of the Sav-ior, the soul - cleans - ing blood, Has

him who from sin set me free, And sing - ing a song full of
gives to his keep - ing his heart! Who walks all se - rene in the
geth - er as chil - dren of God. Our voic - es in praise of the
pow - er to - day o - ver sin, O that the whole world would be

joy, I ex - tol The soul-cleans-ing blood shed for me.
light of his word, In truth that his teach-ings im - part!
Lord we u - nite; He saved us; his glo - ry we laud!
cleansed in that flood, New life and re - demp-tion to win!

The blood of the Sav - ior re - deemed me, In right-eous - ness

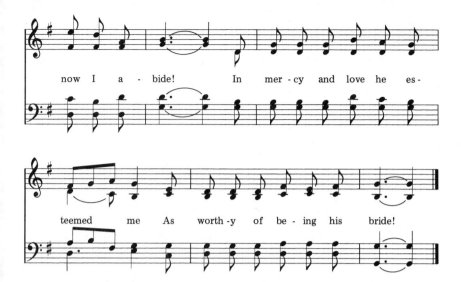

now I a - bide! In mer-cy and love he es-
teemed me As worth-y of be - ing his bride!

EVENING SONG

When at dusk the skies are glowing
Ember-red, and stars are showing
In the firmament their lamps of tender light,
I hear angel voices blending,
Young and sweet, a message sending
To the pilgrim from a land forever bright.

Refrain:
Far beyond the dim horizon,
We shall meet the Savior risen
And shall keep the golden jubilation year.
You, whose pain knew no cessation,
Will forget your tribulation
When the Father's hand shall wipe away each tear.

Isn't now the twilight's burning
But a symbol of the yearning
Of all restless human spirits down the years?
While in stars that shine in glory
Heaven tells its hopeful story,
Ever speaking peace in turmoil, joy in tears.

Sing then, Christian, sing your longing—
Round you all creation thronging—
Earth's disquiet, nature's groaning, sorrow, blight;
Everything on tiptoe singing
Joins the chorus upward winging,
Through the gloom of time to realms of endless light.

Nils W. Lund
tr. Karl A. Olsson

18 Day by Day and with Each Passing Moment

Lina Sandell, 1832-1903
Tr. A. L. Skoog, 1856-1934

BLOTT EN DAG 10.9.10.9.D.
Oscar Ahnfelt, 1813-1882

1 Day by day and with each pass-ing mo-ment, Strength I
2 Ev-'ry day the Lord him-self is near me With a
3 Help me then in ev-'ry trib-u-la-tion So to

find to meet my tri-als here; Trust-ing in my Fa-ther's
spe-cial mer-cy for each hour; All my cares he fain would
trust thy prom-is-es, O Lord, That I lose not faith's sweet

wise be-stow-ment, I've no cause for wor-ry or for fear.
bear, and cheer me, He whose name is Coun-sel-lor and Pow'r.
con-so-la-tion Of-fered me with-in thy ho-ly word.

He whose heart is kind be-yond all meas-ure Gives un-
The pro-tec-tion of his child and treas-ure Is a
Help me, Lord, when toil and trou-ble meet-ing, E'er to

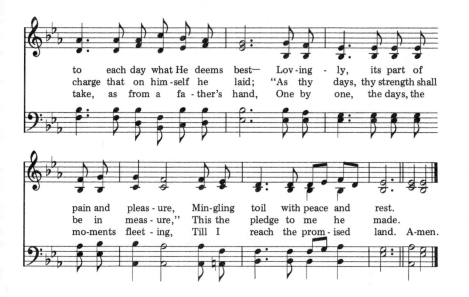

to each day what He deems best— Lov-ing - ly, its part of
charge that on him-self he laid; "As thy days, thy strength shall
take, as from a fa - ther's hand, One by one, the days, the

pain and pleas - ure, Min-gling toil with peace and rest.
be in meas - ure," This the pledge to me he made.
mo-ments fleet - ing, Till I reach the prom-ised land. A-men.

Children of the Heavenly Father 19

Lina Sandell, 1832-1903
Tr. Ernst W. Olson, 1870-1958

TRYGGARE KAN INGEN VARA 8.8.8.8.
Swedish Folk Melody, 1874

1 Chil-dren of the heav'n-ly Fa - ther Safe-ly in his bos - om gath - er;
2 God his own doth tend and nour-ish, In his ho - ly courts they flour-ish;
3 Nei - ther life nor death shall ev - er From the Lord his chil - dren sev - er;
4 Praise the Lord in joy - ful num-bers, Your Pro-tec - tor nev - er slum-bers;
5 Though he giv-eth or he tak -eth, God his chil - dren ne'er for - sak - eth;

Nest-ling bird nor star in heav - en Such a ref - uge e'er was giv - en.
From all e - vil things he spares them, In his might - y arms he bears them.
Un - to them his grace he show-eth, And their sor-rows all he know-eth.
At the will of your De - fend - er Ev - 'ry foe - man must sur - ren-der.
His the lov - ing pur - pose sole - ly To pre - serve them pure and ho - ly.

20 With God as Our Friend

Carl Olof Rosenius, 1816-1868
Tr. Joel Lundeen, 1918-

AHNFELT 11.11.11.6.6.11.
Oscar Ahnfelt, 1813-1882
Harm. by James P. Davies, 1913-

1 With God as our friend, with his Spir - it and Word,
2 In per - il - ous days, filled with storms and with fright,
3 O Shep - herd, a - bide with us, care for us still,

All shar - ing to - geth - er the feast of the Lord,
A band march-es on through thick gloom t'ward the light.
And lead us and guide us and teach us your will,

We face with as - sur - ance the dawn of each day
Not man - y, nor might - y, dis - owned by the world,
Un - til in your heav - en - ly fold we shall sing

And fol - low the shep - herd; and fol - low the shep - herd,
They fol - low their lead - er; they fol - low their lead - er,
Our thanks and our prais - es; our thanks and our prais - es,

Whose voice we have heard and whose will we o - bey.
In con - fi - dent faith, with their ban - ners un - furled.
To God and the Lamb, our re - deem - er and king. A-men.

I Have a Future All Sublime   21

Nils Frykman, 1842-1911
Tr. A. L. Skoog, 1856-1934, St. 1
Tr. Gustaf Frykman, 1873-1953, Sts. 2-5

MIN FRAMTIDSDAG L.M.
Nils Frykman, 1842-1911

1 I have a fu - ture all sub - lime, Be - yond the
2 A pre - cious her - i - tage is mine, In heav - en
3 Praised be the Lord! he planned for me— I need have
4 Now peace and joy with - in me dwell, I sing with
5 Dear Lord, I pray that I may be More whol - ly

realms of space and time, Where my Re - deem - er I shall
kept by love di - vine; What serves me best, while here be -
no anx - i - e - ty; He would a - lone my bur-den
glad - ness, "All is well!" Pro - tect - ed, guid - ed by his
yield - ed un - to thee, While on the way I yet re -

see And sor - row nev - er - more shall be.
low, My Fa - ther will pro - vide, I know.
bear, And make me free from earth - ly care.
might, He leads me to the land of light.
main, Be - fore my heav'n - ly home I gain. A - men.

22   I with Thee Would Begin

Lina Sandell, 1832-1903
Tr. A. Samuel Wallgren, 1885-1940

BEGYNNELSE 12.9.12.9.9.
Wilhelm Theodor Söderberg, 1845-1922
Harm. by James P. Davies, 1913-

1 I with thee would be - gin, O my Sav - ior so dear,
2 I with thee would be - gin— and go forth in thy name,
3 Let thy word all - di - vine be my lamp, in whose light
4 I with thee would be - gin— yea, and hear one more prayer,

On the way that I still must pur - sue; I with thee would be -
Which a - lone doth sal - va - tion be - stow; Fold me close to thy
I may con - stant-ly keep to thy way; And each day wouldst thou
I would close with thee too my brief day; And when day - light has

gin ev - 'ry day grant-ed here, As my ear - nest re - solve I re -
breast, where found joy all who came: There is ref - uge for me too, I
cleanse me a - new, make me white In the blood shed for me on that
failed let me sleep in thy care, Un - til wak - ing thy child thou dost

new: To be and re - main thine for - ev - er.
know, Though all in this world is con - fu - sion.
day The cross thou didst suf - fer, Lord Je - sus.
say, "Come, live with me ev - er in heav - en!" A - men.

Great Hills May Tremble

23

Based on Isaiah 54:10
Lina Sandell, 1832-1903
Tr. E. Lincoln Pearson, 1917-   , Sts. 1,4, alt.
Bryan Jeffery Leech, 1931-   , Sts. 2,3

BERGEN MÅ VIKA 11.10.11.10.
Source Unknown

1 Great hills may trem - ble and moun - tains may crum -ble,
2 Though peace be shat - tered by war's ag - i - ta - tion,
3 Strong to pre - serve us in mo - ments of dan - ger,
4 Teach us, O Lord, thy com - mand-ments to pon - der,

God's lov - ing - kind - ness re - main - eth se - cure;
Though change and ten - sion give birth to great fears,
Strong when frus - tra - tion and frail - ty in - crease;
Help us to heed them wher - ev - er we roam,

Peace he will give to the con - trite and hum - ble:
God still re - mains an un - shak - en foun - da - tion,
Strong to e - quip us for lov - ing the stran - ger,
Wait - ing the day thou shalt call us up yon - der,

Thus saith the Lord— his prom-ise is sure.
Strong to sup - port us through tur - bu - lent years.
Strong where our hu - man re - sourc-es may cease.
Trust-ing thy prom-ise to car - ry us home. A - men.

Words copyright 1950, 1973 by Covenant Press.

24   Thy Holy Wings, Dear Savior

Lina Sandell, 1832-1903
Tr. Ernest Edwin Ryden, 1886-1981

HOLY WINGS 7.6.7.6.D.
Swedish Folk Melody
Harm. by Mark S. Dickey, 1885-1961

1 Thy ho - ly wings, dear Sav - ior, Spread gen - tly o - ver me;
2 Thy par - don, Sav - ior, grant me, And cleanse me in thy blood;

And thru the long night watch - es, I'll rest se - cure in thee.
Give me a will - ing spir - it, A heart both clean and good.

What - ev - er may be - tide me, Be thou my hid - ing place,
O take in - to thy keep - ing Thy chil - dren, great and small,

And let me live and la - bor Each day, Lord, by thy grace.
And, while we sweet - ly slum - ber, En - fold us, one and all. A - men.

Ernest Edwin Ryden, words used by permission.
Harm. used by permission of William K. Provine,
music executor of the estate of Mark S. Dickey.

In the Springtime Fair

25

Lina Sandell, 1832-1903
Tr. Karl A. Olsson, 1913-

SPRINGTIME 8.7.8.7. *with Refrain*
Swedish Folk Melody
Harm. by Norman E. Johnson, 1928-1983

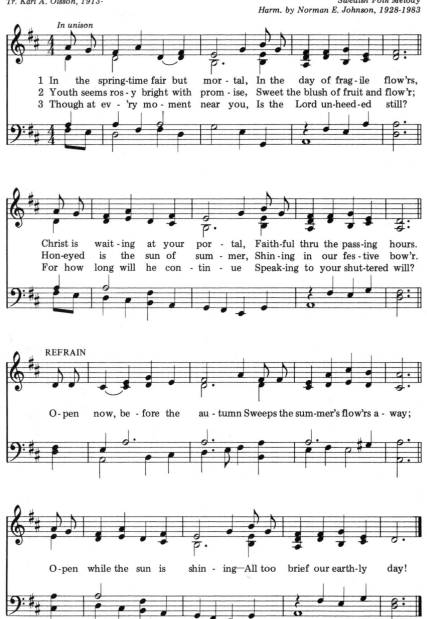

In unison

1 In the spring-time fair but mor - tal, In the day of frag - ile flow'rs,
2 Youth seems ros - y bright with prom - ise, Sweet the blush of fruit and flow'r;
3 Though at ev - 'ry mo - ment near you, Is the Lord un-heed-ed still?

Christ is wait - ing at your por - tal, Faith-ful thru the pass-ing hours.
Hon-eyed is the sun of sum - mer, Shin-ing in our fes - tive bow'r.
For how long will he con - tin - ue Speak-ing to your shut-tered will?

REFRAIN

O-pen now, be - fore the au - tumn Sweeps the sum-mer's flow'rs a - way;

O-pen while the sun is shin - ing—All too brief our earth-ly day!

26 My Soul Now Magnifies the Lord

Based on Luke 1:46-55
Carl Boberg, 1859-1940
Tr. Obed Johnson, 1881-1970

MARIAS LOVSÅNG C.M.D.
Swedish Folk Melody

1 My soul now mag - ni - fies the Lord, With joy his
2 The pow - er of his right - eous arm A - maz - ing
3 His mer - cy is in - deed so great Its length can -
4 His wis - dom can - not be dis-cerned By pow'rs at
5 My soul now mag - ni - fies the Lord, With joy his

praise I sing; For God my Sav - ior un - to me
things has wrought; Earth's might - y ones he has sub -dued,
not be spanned; For those who trust his prom - is - es
our com - mand; But those who tru - ly love the Lord
praise I sing; For God my Sav - ior un - to me

Has done a won - drous thing: This child of dust he
Like dust they've come to naught: The proud of spir - it
His help is near at hand: The cov - e - nant that
Shall know what he has planned: The one whose heart is
Has done a won - drous thing: This child of dust he

rich - ly blessed, His mer - cy fills my soul; For
he has sent With emp - ty souls a - way; To
he has made, As in a for - mer day, For-
filled with pride Will God the Lord bring low; To
set a - part For bless - ed - ness sub - lime; His

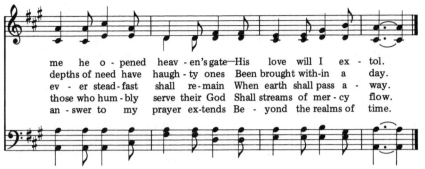

me	he o - pened	heav - en's gate—His	love will I	ex -	tol.
depths of need have	haugh - ty ones	Been brought with-in a	day.
ev - er stead-fast	shall re-main	When earth shall pass a -	way.
those who hum-bly	serve their God	Shall streams of mer - cy	flow.
an - swer to my	prayer ex-tends	Be - yond the realms of	time.

How Wonderful It Is 27

Nils Frykman, 1842-1911
Tr. E. Gustav Johnson, 1893-1974

GEMENSKAP 6.6.7.6.
Nils Frykman, 1842-1911

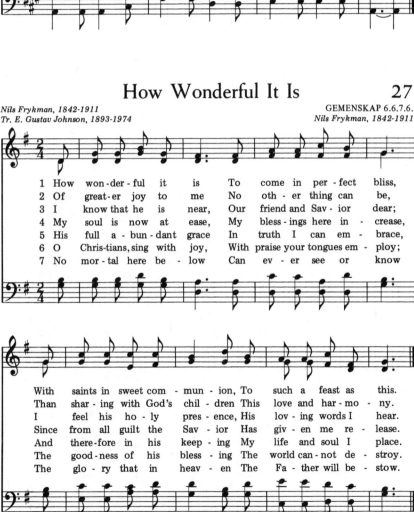

1	How	won-der-ful it	is	To	come in per - fect	bliss,
2	Of	great-er joy to	me	No	oth - er thing can	be,
3	I	know that he is	near,	Our	friend and Sav - ior	dear;
4	My	soul is now at	ease,	My	bless - ings here in -	crease,
5	His	full a - bun - dant	grace	In	truth I can em -	brace,
6	O	Chris-tians, sing with	joy,	With	praise your tongues em -	ploy;
7	No	mor - tal here be -	low	Can	ev - er see or	know

With	saints in sweet com - mun - ion,	To	such a feast as	this.
Than	shar - ing with God's chil - dren	This	love and har - mo -	ny.
I	feel his ho - ly pres - ence,	His	lov - ing words I	hear.
Since	from all guilt the Sav - ior	Has	giv - en me re -	lease.
And	there-fore in his keep - ing	My	life and soul I	place.
The	good-ness of his bless - ing	The	world can-not de -	stroy.
The	glo - ry that in heav - en	The	Fa - ther will be -	stow.

28 Why Should I Be Anxious?

Nils Frykman, 1842-1911
Tr. Aaron Markuson, 1910-

SUNNE 11.8.11.8.
Source unknown

1 Why should I be anx-ious? I have such a friend,
2 Though I am un-worth-y he chose e - ven me,
3 His mer-cy, I know, is suf - fi - cient for me,
4 Each day he is near me, he walks by my side,
5 The pow-er of hell holds no ter - ror for me,
6 Thus on-ward I go to that won-der - ful land,

Who bears in his heart all my woe;
By grace in his king - dom to dwell;
And there - in my soul finds its peace;
His strength nev - er fails, as does mine;
My strong - hold is Is - ra - el's God;
That beau - ti - ful home of the blest;

This friend is the Sav - ior, on him I de-pend—
That grace so a - bun - dant my ref - uge will be—
He chas - tens with love, ev - er pa - tient is he—
In glo - ry with him I at last shall a - bide—
In tri - al and sor - row my ref - uge is he—
Though storms rage in fu - ry, I'm safe in his hand—

His love is e - ter - nal, I know.
Your good - ness, O God, I would tell.
My joys through his bless - ing in - crease.
For that is his prom - ise di - vine.
O Sav - ior, your mer - cy I laud!
I'll en - ter the ha - ven of rest.

O How Blest to Be a Pilgrim

29

Joel Blomqvist, 1840-1930
Lars P. Ollén, 1845-1904
Tr. Signe L. Bennett, 1900-
Tr. Glen V. Wiberg, 1925-

HANSON PLACE 8.7.8.7. *with Refrain*
Robert Lowry, 1826-1899

1 O how blest to be a pil - grim, Guid-ed by the Fa-ther's hand;
2 On this side of Jor-dan's riv - er, Sighs too deep for words are known,
3 There no clouds of dark-ness gath - er, Neith-er sor - row, tears nor woe,
4 Here from loved ones we are part - ed, Earth-ly sor - rows nev - er cease,
5 O may none give up the jour - ney, Left in dark-ness on the shore,

Free at last from ev - 'ry bur - den, We shall en - ter Ca-naan's land.
But we look for bright to - mor - rows In Je - ru - sa - lem our home.
Noth-ing harm-ful e'er shall en - ter, Sin and pain we will not know.
But with - in that glor-ious cit - y, We shall meet a - gain in peace.
May we all at last be gath - ered, When our pil - grim-age is o'er.

REFRAIN

Songs of vic - t'ry there shall greet us, Like the thun-d'ring of a might-y

flood. End-less prais-es be to Je - sus, Who re-deemed us by his blood!

30 We Wait for a Great and Glorious Day

A. L. Skoog, 1856-1934

SKOOG 10.7.10.7. *with Refrain*
A. L. Skoog, 1856-1934

1 We wait for a great and glo-ri-ous day, As man-y as
2 In glo-ry and pow'r our King shall ap-pear, And call to him-
3 For cross-es we've borne then crowns will be giv'n, For tem-pests, e-
4 We know not the day, we know not the hour, When sounds the last

love the Lord, When shad-ows shall flee, and clouds pass a-way, And
self his own; No dis-tance, nor death shall part them as here, Nor
ter-nal calm; For path-way of thorns, rich man-sions in heav'n, For
trump so clear; But loud rings a cry from truth's loft-y tow'r, "The

REFRAIN

weep-ing no more be heard.
sin, with its pains, be known. O won-der-ful day
war-fare, the vic-tor's palm.
day of the Lord is near." O won-der-ful day

that soon may be here! O beau-ti-ful hope
that soon may be here! O beau-ti-ful hope

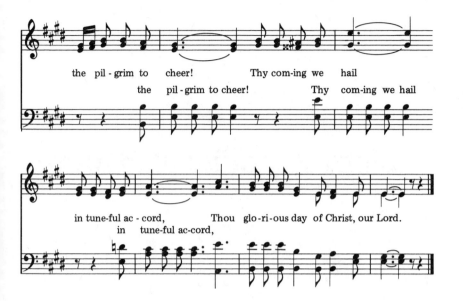

the pil - grim to cheer! Thy com-ing we hail
the pil - grim to cheer! Thy com-ing we hail

in tune-ful ac - cord, Thou glo-ri-ous day of Christ, our Lord.
in tune-ful ac-cord,

The unifying experience of the Mission Friends was salvation. They were one in the Crucified. They gave their freest expression to this in their singing. The name, "läsare," by which Mission Friends were designated in Sweden, emphasized the importance of a devotional reading of the Bible and related literature; it would have been equally correct to call these people "singers." For nothing seems to have brought them closer to a union with Christ than the singing of their hymns. And in the hymns the constantly recurring theme is the friendship of Jesus in the vicissitudes of life and the final "closing" with him when the mists have vanished.

Karl A. Olsson, *By One Spirit*

Sing therefore, you Christians. Rekindle that sacred glow in your souls at the holy altar of song. Sing peace into your own hearts. Sing the doubting and hesitating ones into the presence of Christ. While we are still on this earth our song should continually grow stronger, more joyful, and more rich in meaning. If thus we sing here and now, our song before the throne of God when we have entered into "life more abundant" will be doubly glorious. The Lord entrusts sacred song to human lips. It is a God-given privilege to sing with gladness of heart, as a beautiful testimony to our Christian faith and devotion.

Oscar Lövgren, tr. by Obed Johnson,
from James Davies' *Sing . . . with Understanding*

Classic/Traditional Hymns

Now Thank We All Our God

31

Martin Rinkart, 1586-1649
Tr. Catherine Winkworth, 1827-1878

NUN DANKET 6.7.6.7.6.6.6.6.
Johann Crüger, 1598-1662
Harm. by Felix Mendelssohn, 1809-1847

1 Now thank we all our God With hearts and hands and voic - es,
2 O may this boun-teous God Thru all our life be near us,
3 All praise and thanks to God The Fa - ther now be giv - en,

Who won-drous things has done, In whom his world re - joic - es;
With ev - er joy - ful hearts And bless - ed peace to cheer us;
The Son, and him who reigns With them in high - est heav - en,

Who, from our moth-ers' arms, Has blessed us on our way
And keep us in his grace, And guide us when per - plexed,
The one e - ter - nal God, Whom earth and heav'n a - dore;

With count-less gifts of love, And still is ours to - day.
And free us from all ills In this world and the next.
For thus it was, is now, And shall be ev - er - more. A-men.

32   Praise to the Lord, the Almighty

Joachim Neander, 1650-1680
Tr. Catherine Winkworth, 1827-1878, alt.

LOBE DEN HERREN 14.14.4.7.8.
"Stralsund Gesangbuch," 1665

1 Praise to the Lord, the Al - might-y, the King of cre - a - tion!
2 Praise to the Lord, who o'er all things so won-drous-ly reign - eth,
3 Praise to the Lord, who doth pros-per thy work and de - fend thee;
4 Praise to the Lord! O let all that is in me a - dore him!

O my soul, praise him, for he is thy health and sal - va - tion!
Shel-ters thee un - der his wings, yea, so gen - tly sus - tain - eth!
Sure - ly his good-ness and mer - cy here dai - ly at - tend thee.
All that hath life and breath, come now with prais-es be - fore him.

All ye who hear, Now to his tem - ple draw near;
Hast thou not seen How thy de - sires e'er have been
Pon - der a - new What the Al - might - y can do,
Let the A - men Sound from his peo - ple a - gain:

Join me in glad ad - o - ra - tion!
Grant-ed in what he or - dain - eth?
If with his love he be - friend thee.
Glad - ly for aye we a - dore him. A - men.

O Worship the King All Glorious Above 33

Robert Grant, 1779-1838

LYONS 10.10.11.11.
Adapted from Johann Michael Haydn, 1737-1806

1 O wor - ship the King all glo - rious a - bove,
2 O tell of his might and sing of his grace,
3 Thy boun - ti - ful care what tongue can re - cite?
4 Frail chil - dren of dust, and fee - ble as frail,

And grate - ful - ly sing his won - der - ful love;
Whose robe is the light, whose can - o - py space;
It breathes in the air, it shines in the light,
In thee do we trust, nor find thee to fail;

Our Shield and De - fend - er, the An - cient of Days,
His char - iots of wrath the deep thun-der - clouds form,
It streams from the hills, it de - scends to the plain,
Thy mer - cies how ten - der, how firm to the end,

Pa - vil - ioned in splen-dor and gird - ed with praise.
And dark is his path on the wings of the storm.
And sweet-ly dis - tills in the dew and the rain.
Our Mak - er, De - fend - er, Re - deem - er and Friend. A - men.

34 Praise, My Soul, the King of Heaven

Based on Psalm 103
Henry Francis Lyte, 1793-1847, alt.

PRAISE MY SOUL 8.7.8.7.8.7.
John Goss, 1800-1880

1 Praise, my soul, the King of heav - en, To his feet your
2 Praise him for his grace and fa - vor To our fore-bears
3 Fa - ther - like he tends and spares us; Well our fee - ble
4 An - gels, help us to a - dore him, Who be - hold him

trib - ute bring; Ran - somed, healed, re - stored, for - giv - en,
in dis - tress; Praise him, still the same as ev - er,
frame he knows; In his hands he gen - tly bears us,
face to face; Sun and moon, bow down be - fore him,

Ev - er - more his prais - es sing: Al - le - lu - ia!
Slow to chide, and swift to bless: Al - le - lu - ia!
Res - cues us from all our foes. Al - le - lu - ia!
Dwell-ers all in time and space. Al - le - lu - ia!

Al - le - lu - ia! Praise the ev - er - last - ing King.
Al - le - lu - ia! Glo - rious in his faith-ful - ness.
Al - le - lu - ia! Wide - ly yet his mer - cy flows.
Al - le - lu - ia! Praise with us the God of grace. A - men.

Immortal, Invisible, God Only Wise 35

Walter Chalmers Smith, 1824-1908, alt.

ST. DENIO 11.11.11.11.
Welsh Melody
John Roberts' "Caniadau y Cyssegr," 1839

1 Im - mor - tal, in - vis - i - ble, God on - ly wise,
2 Un - rest - ing, un - hast - ing, and si - lent as light,
3 To all, life thou giv - est, to both great and small;
4 Great Fa - ther of glo - ry, pure Fa - ther of light,

In light in - ac - ces - si - ble hid from our eyes,
Nor want - ing, nor wast - ing, thou rul - est in might;
In all life thou liv - est, the true life of all;
Thine an - gels a - dore thee, all veil - ing their sight;

Most bless - ed, most glo - rious, the An - cient of Days,
Thy jus - tice like moun - tains high soar - ing a - bove
We blos - som and flour - ish as leaves on the tree,
All praise we would ren - der: O help us to see

Al - might-y, vic - to - rious, thy great name we praise.
Thy clouds, which are foun - tains of good - ness and love.
And with - er and per - ish— but naught chang-eth thee.
'Tis on - ly the splen-dor of light hid - eth thee. A - men.

36   Holy, Holy, Holy! Lord God Almighty!

Reginald Heber, 1783-1826

NICAEA *Irregular*
John B. Dykes, 1823-1876
Descant by David McK. Williams, 1887-1978

Descant for stanza 4

Ho - - - - - - - - - ly,

1 Ho - ly, ho - ly,   ho - ly!   Lord   God Al - might - y!
2 Ho - ly, ho - ly,   ho - ly!   all the saints a - dore   thee,
3 Ho - ly, ho - ly,   ho - ly!   tho the dark - ness hide   thee,
4 Ho - ly, ho - ly,   ho - ly!   Lord   God Al - might - y!

Ho - - - - - - - - - ly,

Ear - ly in the   morn - ing our   song shall rise to   thee;
Cast - ing down their gold - en crowns a - round the glass - y   sea;
Tho   the eye made blind by sin thy   glo - ry may not   see;
All   thy works shall praise thy name in   earth and sky and   sea;

Ho - - - - - - - - - ly,

Ho - ly, ho - ly,   ho - ly!   mer - ci - ful and   might - y!
Cher - u - bim and   ser - a - phim   fall - ing down be - fore   thee,
On - ly thou art   ho - ly—   there   is none be - side   thee
Ho - ly, ho - ly,   ho - ly!   mer - ci - ful and   might - y!

Descant from *34 Hymn Tune Descants*, copyright 1948
by the H.W. Gray Co., Inc. Used by permission.

God in three per-sons, bless-ed Trin - i - ty! A-men.

God in three per - sons, bless-ed Trin - i - ty!
Who wert, and art, and ev - er-more shalt be.
Per - fect in pow'r, in love and pu - ri - ty.
God in three per - sons, bless-ed Trin - i - ty! A - men.

O God, Our Help in Ages Past   37

Based on Psalm 90
Isaac Watts, 1674-1748

ST. ANNE C.M.
Attr. to William Croft, 1678-1727

1 O God, our help in a - ges past, Our hope for years to come,
2 Un - der the shad -ow of thy throne Thy saints have dwelt se - cure;
3 Be - fore the hills in or-der stood Or earth re - ceived her frame,
4 A thou-sand a - ges in thy sight Are like an eve - ning gone,
5 Time, like an ev - er roll-ing stream, Soon bears us all a - way;
6 O God, our help in a - ges past, Our hope for years to come,

Our shel -ter from the storm-y blast, And our e - ter - nal home:
Suf - fi - cient is thine arm a - lone, And our de-fense is sure.
From ev - er - last - ing thou art God, To end-less years the same.
Short as the watch that ends the night Be - fore the ris - ing sun.
We fly, for - got - ten, as a dream Dies at the open-ing day.
Be thou our guide while life shall last, And our e - ter - nal home. A-men.

38   And Can It Be That I Should Gain

Charles Wesley, 1707-1788

SAGINA 8.8.8.8.8.8. *with Refrain*
Thomas Campbell, 1777-1844

1 And can it be that I should gain An in - t'rest in the Sav - ior's blood? Died he for me, who caused his pain? For me, who him to death pur - sued? A - maz - ing love! how can it be That thou, my God, shouldst die for me?

2 He left his Fa - ther's throne a - bove, So free, so in - fi - nite his grace! Emp - tied him - self of all but love, And bled for A - dam's help - less race! 'Tis mer - cy all, im - mense and free, For, O my God, it found out me.

3 Long my im - pris - oned spir - it lay Fast bound in sin and na - ture's night. Thine eye dif - fused a quick - 'ning ray; I woke— the dun - geon flamed with light! My chains fell off, my heart was free, I rose, went forth, and fol - lowed thee.

4 No con-dem - na - tion now I dread: Je - sus, and all in him, is mine! A - live in him, my liv - ing Head, And clothed in right - eous - ness di - vine, Bold I ap - proach th'e - ter - nal throne, And claim the crown, thru Christ my own.

REFRAIN

A - maz - ing love! how can it be

A - maz - ing love! how can it be

That thou, my God, shouldst die for me! A - men.

O for a Thousand Tongues to Sing   39

Charles Wesley, 1707-1788

AZMON C.M.
Carl G. Gläser, 1784-1829
Mason's "Modern Psalmody," 1839

1 O   for a thou-sand tongues to sing   My great Re-deem-er's praise,
2 My   gra-cious Mas-ter and my God, As - sist me to pro - claim,
3 The name of Je - sus charms our fears, And bids our sor-rows cease,
4 He   breaks the pow'r of can-celled sin, He sets the pris-'ner free;
5 Glo - ry to God and praise and love Be ev - er, ev - er giv'n

The glo-ries of my God and King, The tri-umphs of his grace!
To spread thru all the earth a-broad The hon-ors of your name.
'Tis mu - sic in the sin - ner's ears, 'Tis life and health and peace.
His blood can make the foul-est clean, His blood a-vailed for me.
By saints be - low and saints a-bove, The Church in earth and heav'n. A - men.

40   Come, Christians, Join to Sing

Christian Henry Bateman, 1813-1889

SPANISH HYMN 6.6.6.6.D.
Source unknown
Harm. by A. Royce Eckhardt, 1937-

1 Come, Chris-tians, join to sing— Al - le - lu - ia! A - men!
2 Come, lift your hearts on high— Al - le - lu - ia! A - men!
3 Praise yet our Christ a - gain— Al - le - lu - ia! A - men!

Loud praise to Christ our King— Al - le - lu - ia! A - men!
Let prais - es fill the sky— Al - le - lu - ia! A - men!
Life shall not end the strain— Al - le - lu - ia! A - men!

Let all, with heart and voice, Be - fore his throne re-joice;
He is our guide and friend, To us he'll con - de-scend;
On heav-en's bliss - ful shore His good-ness we'll a - dore,

Praise is his gra-cious choice: Al - le - lu - ia! A - men!
His love shall nev - er end: Al - le - lu - ia! A - men!
Sing - ing for - ev - er - more, "Al - le - lu - ia! A - men!"

Crown Him with Many Crowns

Matthew Bridges, 1800-1894
Godfrey Thring, 1823-1903, St. 3

DIADEMATA S.M.D.
George J. Elvey, 1816-1893

1 Crown him with man-y crowns, The Lamb up-on his throne:
2 Crown him the Lord of love: Be-hold his hands and side,
3 Crown him the Lord of life: Who tri-umphed o'er the grave,
4 Crown him the Lord of heav'n: One with the Fa-ther known,
5 Crown him the Lord of years: The po-ten-tate of time,

Hark! how the heav'n-ly an-them drowns All mu-sic but its own!
Rich wounds, yet vis-i-ble a-bove, In beau-ty glo-ri-fied;
Who rose vic-to-rious to the strife For those he came to save;
One with the Spir-it through him giv'n From yon-der glo-rious throne.
Cre-a-tor of the roll-ing spheres, In-ef-fa-bly sub-lime.

A-wake, my soul, and sing Of him who died for thee; And
No an-gel in the sky Can ful-ly bear that sight, But
His glo-ries now we sing, Who died and rose on high, Who
To thee be end-less praise, For thou for us hast died; Be
All hail, Re-deem-er, hail! For thou hast died for me; Thy

hail him as thy match-less King Thru all e-ter-ni-ty.
down-ward bends a won-d'ring eye At mys-ter-ies so bright.
died e-ter-nal life to bring, And lives that death may die.
thou, O Lord, thru end-less days A-dored and mag-ni-fied.
praise and glo-ry shall not fail Thru-out e-ter-ni-ty. A-men.

42 All Hail the Power of Jesus' Name!

Edward Perronet, 1726-1792
Alt. by John Rippon, 1751-1836

CORONATION C.M.
Oliver Holden, 1765-1844

1 All hail the pow'r of Je - sus' name! Let an - gels pros - trate fall;
2 You cho - sen seed of Is - rael's race, You ran - somed from the fall,
3 Let ev - 'ry kin - dred, ev - 'ry tribe, On this ter - res - trial ball,
4 O that with yon - der sa - cred throng We at his feet may fall!

Bring forth the roy - al di - a - dem, And crown him Lord of all; Bring
Hail him who saves you by his grace, And crown him Lord of all; Hail
To him all maj - es - ty as - cribe, And crown him Lord of all; To
We'll join the ev - er - last - ing song, And crown him Lord of all; We'll

forth the roy - al di - a - dem, And crown him Lord of all!
him who saves you by his grace, And crown him Lord of all!
him all maj - es - ty as - cribe, And crown him Lord of all!
join the ev - er - last - ing song, And crown him Lord of all! A - men.

43 Beautiful Savior! King of Creation!

From "Münster Gesangbuch," 1677

CRUSADERS' HYMN 5.5.7.5.5.8.
Silesian Folksong

1 Beau - ti - ful Sav - ior! King of cre - a - tion! Son of
2 Fair are the mead - ows, Fair are the wood - lands, Robed in
3 Fair is the sun - shine, Fair is the moon - light, Bright the
4 Beau - ti - ful Sav - ior! Lord of the na - tions! Son of

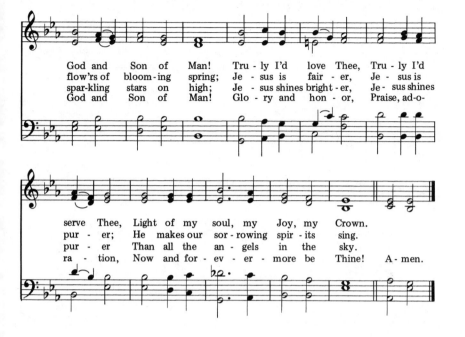

God and Son of Man! Tru - ly I'd love Thee, Tru - ly I'd
flow'rs of bloom-ing spring; Je - sus is fair - er, Je - sus is
spar-kling stars on high; Je - sus shines bright - er, Je - sus shines
God and Son of Man! Glo - ry and hon - or, Praise, ad-o-

serve Thee, Light of my soul, my Joy, my Crown.
pur - er; He makes our sor - rowing spir - its sing.
pur - er Than all the an - gels in the sky.
ra - tion, Now and for - ev - er - more be Thine! A - men.

A Christian hymn is a lyric poem, reverently and devotionally con-
ceived, which is designed to be sung and which expresses the worshiper's
attitude toward God, or God's purposes in human life. It should be sim-
ple and metrical in form, genuinely emotional, poetic, and literary in
style, spiritual in quality, and in its ideas so direct and so immediately
apparent as to unify a congregation while singing it.

The Hymn Society of America

44   Alleluia! Sing to Jesus!

William C. Dix, 1837-1898

HYFRYDOL 8.7.8.7.D.
Rowland H. Prichard, 1811-1887

1 Al - le - lu - ia! sing to Je - sus! His the scep - ter,
his the throne; Al - le - lu - ia! his the tri - umph, His the
vic - to - ry a - lone; Hark! the songs of peace - ful Zi - on
Thun - der like a might - y flood; Je - sus, out of ev - 'ry
na - tion Has re - deemed us by his blood.

2 Al - le - lu - ia! not as or - phans Are we left in
sor - row now; Al - le - lu - ia! he is near us, Faith be-
lieves, nor ques - tions how: Though the cloud from sight re - ceived him
When the for - ty days were o'er, Shall our hearts for - get his
prom - ise, "I am with you ev - er - more"?

3 Al - le - lu - ia! Bread of Heav - en, You on earth our
food, our stay! Al - le - lu - ia! here the sin - ful Flee to
you from day to day; In - ter - ces - sor, friend of sin - ners,
Earth's Re - deem - er, plead for me, Where the songs of all the
sin - less Sweep a - cross the crys - tal sea. A - men.

Sing Hallelujah, Praise the Lord! 45

John Swertner, 1746-1813

BECHLER 8.6.8.6.8.8.8.6.
John C. Bechler, 1784-1857

1 Sing hal - le - lu - jah, praise the Lord! Sing with a cheer-ful voice;
2 There we to all e - ter - ni - ty Shall join an - gel - ic lays

Ex - alt our God with one ac-cord, And in his name re - joice.
And sing in per-fect har - mo-ny To God our Sav-ior's praise;

Ne'er cease to sing, you ran-somed host, Praise Fa-ther, Son, and Ho - ly Ghost,
He has re-deemed us by his blood, And made us kings and priests to God;

Un - til in realms of end - less light Your prais-es shall u - nite.
For us, for us, the Lamb was slain! O praise the Lord! A - men.

46   We Come, O Christ, to Thee

E. Margaret Clarkson, 1915-

DARWALL'S 148th 6.6.6.6.8.8.
John Darwall, 1731-1789

1 We come, O Christ, to thee, True son of God and man, By whom all things con - sist, In whom all life be - gan: In thee a - lone we live and move And have our be - ing, in thy love.

2 Thou art the way to God, Thy blood our ran - som paid; In thee we face our Judge And Mak - er un - a - fraid: Be - fore the throne ab - solved we stand, Thy love has met thy law's de - mand.

3 Thou art the liv - ing truth! All wis - dom dwells in thee, The source of ev - 'ry skill, E - ter - nal Ver - i - ty: Thou great "I am!" in thee we rest, True an - swer to our ev - 'ry quest.

4 Thou on - ly art true life, To know thee is to live The more a - bun - dant life That earth can nev - er give: O ris - en Lord! we live in thee And thou in us e - ter - nal - ly!

5 We wor - ship thee, Lord Christ, Our Sav - ior and our King, To thee our youth and strength A - dor - ing - ly we bring: So fill our hearts, that men may see Thy life in us and turn to thee! A - men!

God of Grace and God of Glory

47

Harry Emerson Fosdick, 1878-1969

CWM RHONDDA 8.7.8.7.8.7.
John Hughes, 1873-1932

1 God of grace and God of glo - ry,
2 Lo! the hosts of e - vil round us
3 Cure your chil - dren's war - ring mad - ness;
4 Save us from weak res - ig - na - tion

On your peo - ple
Scorn the Christ, as-
Bend our pride to
To the e - vils

pour your power; Crown your an - cient church's sto - ry, Bring her bud to
sail his ways! From the fears that long have bound us, Free our hearts to
your con - trol; Shame our want - on, self - ish glad - ness, Rich in things and
we de - plore; Let the search for your sal - va - tion Be our glo - ry

glo - rious flower. Grant us wis - dom, Grant us cour - age,
faith and praise. Grant us wis - dom, Grant us cour - age,
poor in soul. Grant us wis - dom, Grant us cour - age,
ev - er - more. Grant us wis - dom, Grant us cour - age,

For the fac - ing of this hour, For the fac - ing of this hour.
For the liv - ing of these days, For the liv - ing of these days.
Lest we miss your king-dom's goal, Lest we miss your king-dom's goal.
Serv - ing you whom we a - dore, Serv - ing you whom we a - dore. A-men.

Words used by permission of Elinor Fosdick Downs.
Music ©by Mrs. Dily Webb c/o Mechanical Copyright Protection
Society Limited, and reproduced by permission of the legal repre-
sentatives of the composer, who reserve all rights therein.

48 How Firm a Foundation

"K" in John Rippon's "Selection of Hymns," 1787, alt.

FOUNDATION 11.11.11.11.
American Melody
Harm. by A. Royce Eckhardt, 1937-

In unison

1 How firm a foun - da - tion, ye saints of the Lord,
2 "Fear not, I am with thee, O be not dis - mayed,
3 "When through fier - y tri - als thy path - way shall lie,
4 "The soul that on Je - sus hath leaned for re - pose

Is laid for your faith in his ex - cel - lent word!
For I am thy God, I will still give thee aid;
My grace, all - suf - fi - cient, shall be thy sup - ply;
I will not, I will not de - sert to his foes:

What more can he say than to you he hath said,
I'll strength - en thee, help thee, and cause thee to stand,
The flame shall not hurt thee—I on - ly de - sign
That soul, though all hell should en - deav - or to shake,

To you, who for ref - uge to Je - sus have fled?
Up - held by my gra - cious, om - ni - po - tent hand.
Thy dross to con - sume and thy gold to re - fine.
I'll nev - er, no, nev - er, no, nev - er for - sake!"

A Mighty Fortress Is Our God

49

Based on Psalm 46
Martin Luther, 1483-1546
Tr. Frederick H. Hedge, 1805-1890

EIN' FESTE BURG 8.7.8.7.6.6.6.6.7.
Martin Luther, 1483-1546

1 A might-y for - tress is our God, A bul-wark nev - er fail - ing;
2 Did we in our own strength con-fide, Our striv-ing would be los - ing,
3 And tho this world, with dev - ils filled, Should threat-en to un-do us,
4 That word a - bove all earth-ly pow'rs, No thanks to them, a-bid - eth;

Our help-er he a - mid the flood Of mor-tal ills pre - vail - ing.
Were not the right man on our side, The man of God's own choos - ing.
We will not fear, for God hath willed His truth to tri - umph thru us.
The Spir - it and the gifts are ours Thru him who with us sid - eth.

For still our an-cient foe Doth seek to work us woe—His craft and pow'r are
Dost ask who that may be? Christ Je-sus, it is he— Lord Sab - a - oth his
The prince of dark-ness grim, We trem-ble not for him— His rage we can en-
Let goods and kin-dred go, This mor-tal life al - so— The bod - y they may

great, And, armed with cru-el hate, On earth is not his e - qual.
name, From age to age the same, And he must win the bat - tle.
dure, For lo, his doom is sure: One lit - tle word shall fell him.
kill; God's truth a - bid - eth still: His king-dom is for - ev - er. A-men.

50 Great Is Thy Faithfulness

Based on Lamentations 3:22,23
Thomas O. Chisholm, 1866-1960

FAITHFULNESS 11.10.11.10. *with Refrain*
William M. Runyan, 1870-1957

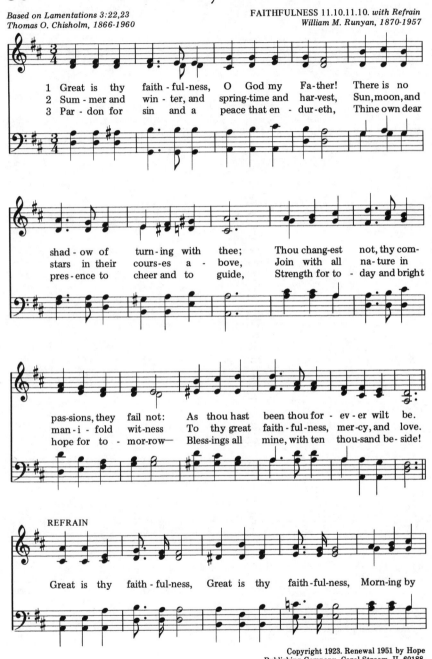

1 Great is thy   faith - ful - ness,   O   God my   Fa - ther!   There is no
2 Sum - mer and   win - ter, and   spring-time and   har-vest,   Sun, moon, and
3 Par - don for   sin   and a   peace that en - dur-eth,   Thine own dear

shad - ow of   turn - ing with   thee;   Thou chang-est   not, thy com-
stars   in their   cours-es   a - bove,   Join with all   na - ture in
pres - ence to   cheer and to   guide,   Strength for to - day and bright

pas-sions, they   fail not: As   thou hast   been thou for - ev - er wilt   be.
man - i - fold   wit-ness   To   thy great   faith - ful - ness,   mer-cy, and   love.
hope for to - mor-row—   Bless-ings all   mine, with ten   thou-sand be-side!

REFRAIN

Great is thy   faith - ful-ness,   Great is thy   faith-ful-ness,   Morn-ing by

morn-ing new mer-cies I see; All I have need-ed thy

hand hath pro-vid-ed— Great is thy faith-ful-ness, Lord, un-to me! A-men.

O Master, Let Me Walk with Thee 51

Washington Gladden, 1836-1918

MARYTON L.M.
H. Percy Smith, 1825-1898

1 O Mas-ter, let me walk with thee In low-ly
2 Help me the slow of heart to move By some clear,
3 Teach me thy pa-tience; still with thee In clos-er,
4 In hope that sends a shin-ing ray Far down the

paths of serv-ice free; Tell me thy se-cret— help me
win-ning word of love; Teach me the way-ward feet to
dear-er com-pa-ny, In work that keeps faith sweet and
fu-ture's broad-'ning way, In peace that on-ly thou canst

bear The strain of toil, the fret of care.
stay, And guide them in the home-ward way.
strong, In trust that tri-umphs o-ver wrong.
give, With thee, O Mas-ter, let me live. A-men.

52 Be Thou My Vision

Ancient Irish
Tr. Mary E. Byrne, 1880-1931
Versified by Eleanor H. Hull, 1860-1935

SLANE 10.10.9.10.
Irish Melody
Harm. by Carlton R. Young, 1926-

In unison

1 Be thou my vi - sion, O Lord of my heart,
2 Be thou my wis - dom, and thou my true word,
3 Rich - es I heed not, nor man's emp - ty praise,
4 High King of heav - en, my vic - to - ry won,

Naught be all else to me, save that thou art;
I ev - er with thee and thou with me, Lord;
Thou mine in - her - i - tance, now and al - ways;
May I reach heav - en's joys, O bright heav'n's Sun!

Thou my best thought, by day or by night,
Thou my great Fa - ther, and I thy true son,
Thou and thou on - ly, first in my heart,
Heart of my own heart, what - ev - er be - fall,

Wak - ing or sleep - ing, thy pres - ence my light.
Thou in me dwell - ing, and I with thee one.
High King of heav - en, my treas - ure thou art.
Still be my vi - sion, O Rul - er of all. A - men.

Words from <u>The Poem Book of the Gael</u>; Selected and edited by Eleanor Hull. Used by permission of the Editor's Literary Estate and Chatto & Windus, Ltd. Harm. copyright © 1964 by Abingdon Press. Used by permission.

Lead On, O King Eternal

53

Ernest W. Shurtleff, 1862-1917

LANCASHIRE 7.6.7.6.D.
Henry T. Smart, 1813-1879

1 Lead on, O King e-ter-nal, The day of march has come;
2 Lead on, O King e-ter-nal, Till sin's fierce war shall cease,
3 Lead on, O King e-ter-nal, We fol-low not with fears,

Hence-forth in fields of con-quest Thy tents shall be our home.
And ho-li-ness shall whis-per The sweet a-men of peace.
For glad-ness breaks like morn-ing Wher-e'er thy face ap-pears.

Through days of prep-a-ra-tion Thy grace has made us strong,
For not with swords' loud clash-ing, Nor roll of stir-ring drums—
Thy cross is lift-ed o'er us, We jour-ney in its light;

And now, O King e-ter-nal, We lift our bat-tle song.
With deeds of love and mer-cy The heav'n-ly king-dom comes.
The crown a-waits the con-quest: Lead on, O God of might. A-men.

54   My Hope Is Built on Nothing Less

Edward Mote, 1797-1874

MELITA 8.8.8.8.8.8.
John B. Dykes, 1823-1876

1 My hope is built on noth-ing less Than Je-sus' blood and
2 When dark-ness veils his love-ly face, I rest on his un-
3 His oath, his cov-e-nant, his blood, Sup-port me in the
4 When he shall come with trum-pet sound, O may I then in

right-eous-ness; I dare not trust the sweet-est frame,
chang-ing grace; In ev-'ry high and storm-y gale,
whelm-ing flood; When all a-round my soul gives way,
him be found: Dressed in his right-eous-ness a-lone,

But whol-ly lean on Je-sus' name. On Christ, the sol-id
My an-chor holds with-in the veil. On Christ, the sol-id
He then is all my hope and stay. On Christ, the sol-id
Fault-less to stand be-fore the throne. On Christ, the sol-id

Rock, I stand: All oth-er ground is sink-ing sand.
Rock, I stand: All oth-er ground is sink-ing sand.
Rock, I stand: All oth-er ground is sink-ing sand.
Rock, I stand: All oth-er ground is sink-ing sand.

The Church's One Foundation 55

Samuel J. Stone, 1839-1900

AURELIA 7.6.7.6.D.
Samuel S. Wesley, 1810-1876

1 The Church-'s one foun - da - tion Is Je - sus Christ her Lord;
2 E - lect from ev - 'ry na - tion Yet one o'er all the earth,
3 'Mid toil and trib - u - la - tion And tu - mult of her war,
4 Yet she on earth has un - ion With God, the Three in One,

She is his new cre - a - tion By wa - ter and the word.
Her char - ter of sal - va - tion, One Lord, one faith, one birth;
She waits the con - sum - ma - tion Of peace for ev - er - more;
And mys - tic sweet com - mun - ion With those whose rest is won.

From heav'n he came and sought her To be his ho - ly bride;
One ho - ly name she bless - es, Par - takes one ho - ly food,
Till with the vi - sion glo - rious, Her long - ing eyes are blest,
O hap - py ones and ho - ly! Lord, give us grace that we

With his own blood he bought her, And for her life he died.
And to one hope she press - es, With ev - ery grace en - dued.
And the great Church vic - to - rious Shall be the Church at rest.
Like them, the meek and low - ly, On high may dwell with thee. A-men.

56 For All the Saints

William W. How, 1823-1897

SINE NOMINE 10.10.10. *with Alleluias*
Ralph Vaughan Williams, 1872-1958

In unison

1 For all the saints who from their la - bors rest, Who
2 Thou wast their rock, their for - tress, and their might, Thou,
3 O may thy sol - diers, faith - ful, true, and bold,
4 O blest com - mu - nion, fel - low - ship di - vine!
5 But lo! there breaks a yet more glo - rious day: The
6 From earth's wide bounds, from o - cean's far - thest coast, Thru

thee by faith be - fore the world con - fessed, Thy
Lord, their cap - tain in the well - fought fight;
Fight as the saints who no - bly fought of old, And
We fee - bly strug - gle, they in glo - ry shine; Yet
saints tri - um - phant rise in bright ar - ray; The
gates of pearl streams in the count - less host,

name, O Je - sus, be for - ev - er blest:
Thou, in the dark - ness drear, their one true light:
win with them the vic - tor's crown of gold:
all are one in thee, for all are thine:
King of glo - ry pass - es on his way:
Sing - ing to Fa - ther, Son, and Ho - ly Ghost:

Al - le - lu - ia! Al - le - lu - ia! A-men.

The days were not long enough as I meditated, and found wonderful
delight in meditating, upon the depths of thy design for the salvation of
the human race. I wept at the beauty of thy hymns and canticles, and
was powerfully moved at the sweet sound of thy Church's singing.
Those sounds flowed into my ears, and the truth streamed into my
heart: so that my feeling of devotion overflowed, and the tears ran from
my eyes, and I was happy in them. It was only a little while before that
the church of Milan had begun to practice this kind of consolation and
exultation, to the great joy of the brethren singing together with heart
and voice. . . . The custom has been retained from that day to this, and
has been imitated by many, indeed, in almost all congregations through-
out the world.

St. Augustine, *Confessions*

Therefore, since we are surrounded by so great a cloud of witnesses, let
us also lay aside every weight, and sin which clings so closely, and let us
run with perseverance the race that is set before us, looking to Jesus the
pioneer and perfector of our faith, who for the joy that was set before
him endured the cross, despising the shame, and is seated at the right
hand of the throne of God.

Hebrews 12:1,2

57 Come, Thou Fount of Every Blessing

Robert Robinson, 1735-1790

NETTLETON 8.7.8.7.D.
John Wyeth, 1770-1858

1 Come, thou Fount of ev - 'ry bless-ing, Tune my heart to sing thy grace;
2 Here I raise mine Eb-en - e - zer,* Hith-er by thy help I'm come;
3 O to grace how great a debt-or Dai-ly I'm con-strained to be!

Streams of mer - cy, nev-er ceas - ing, Call for songs of loud-est praise.
And I hope, by thy good pleas-ure, Safe-ly to ar - rive at home.
Let thy good-ness, like a fet - ter, Bind my wan-d'ring heart to thee:

Teach me some me - lo-dious son - net, Sung by flam-ing tongues a - bove;
Je - sus sought me when a stran-ger, Wan-d'ring from the fold of God;
Prone to wan - der, Lord, I feel it, Prone to leave the God I love:

Praise the mount! I'm fixed up - on it, Mount of thy re-deem-ing love.
He, to res - cue me from dan-ger, In - ter - posed his pre-cious blood.
Here's my heart, O take and seal it, Seal it for thy courts a - bove. A - men.

*I Sam. 7:12

Gospel Hymns

58 Praise Him! Praise Him!

Fanny J. Crosby, 1820-1915   *Chester G. Allen, 1838-1878*

1 Praise him! praise him! Je-sus our bless-ed Re-deem-er! Sing, O Earth, his
2 Praise him! praise him! Je-sus our bless-ed Re-deem-er! For our sins he
3 Praise him! praise him! Je-sus our bless-ed Re-deem-er! Heav'n-ly por-tals

won-der-ful love pro-claim! Hail him! hail him! high-est arch-an-gels in glo-ry;
suffered, and bled, and died; He our Rock, our hope of e-ter-nal sal-va-tion,
loud with ho-san-nas ring! Je-sus, Sav-ior, reign-eth for-ev-er and ev-er;

Strength and hon-or give to his ho-ly name! Like a shep-herd, Je-sus will
Hail him! hail him! Je-sus the Cru-ci-fied. Sound his prais-es! Je-sus, who
Crown him! crown him! Prophet, and Priest and King! Christ is com-ing! o-ver the

REFRAIN

guard his chil-dren, In his arms he car-ries them all day long:
bore our sor-rows, Love unbounded, wonderful, deep and strong: Praise him! praise him!
world vic-to-rious, Pow'r and glo-ry un-to the Lord be-long:

tell of his ex-cel-lent great-ness; Praise him! praise him! ev-er in joy-ful song!

Come, We That Love the Lord

59

Isaac Watts, 1674-1748
Robert Lowry, 1826-1899, Refrain

MARCHING TO ZION S.M. *with Refrain*
Robert Lowry, 1826-1899

1 Come, we that love the Lord, And let our joys be known; Join
2 Let those re - fuse to sing Who nev - er knew our God; But
3 Then let our songs a-bound And ev - 'ry tear be dry; We're

in a song with sweet ac-cord, Join in a song with sweet ac-cord
chil-dren of the heav'n-ly King, But chil-dren of the heav'n-ly King
march-ing thru Em - man-uel's ground, We're march-ing thru Em - man-uel's ground

And thus sur - round the throne, And thus sur-round the throne.
May speak their joys a-broad, May speak their joys a - broad.
To fair - er worlds on high, To fair - er worlds on high.

REFRAIN

We're march-ing to Zi - on, Beau-ti-ful, beau-ti-ful Zi - on; We're

march-ing up-ward to Zi - on, The beau-ti-ful cit - y of God.

60 To God Be the Glory

Fanny J. Crosby, 1820-1915

TO GOD BE THE GLORY 11.11.11.11. *with Refrain*
William H. Doane, 1832-1915

1 To God be the glo-ry—great things he hath done! So loved he the
2 O per-fect re-demp-tion, the pur-chase of blood, To ev-'ry be-
3 Great things he hath taught us, great things he hath done, And great our re-

world that he gave us his Son, Who yield-ed his life an a-
liev-er the prom-ise of God; The vil-est of-fen-der who
joic-ing thru Je-sus the Son; But pu-rer, and high-er, and

tone-ment for sin, And o-pened the life-gate that all may go in.
tru-ly be-lieves, That mo-ment from Je-sus a par-don re-ceives.
great-er will be Our won-der, our trans-port, when Je-sus we see.

REFRAIN

Praise the Lord, praise the Lord, Let the earth hear his voice! Praise the

Lord, praise the Lord, Let the peo-ple re-joice! O come to the Fa-ther thru

Je-sus the Son, And give him the glo-ry—great things he hath done!

SING ALL. See that you join with the congregation as frequently as you can. Let not a slight degree of weakness or weariness hinder you. If it is a cross to you, take it up, and you will find it a blessing.

SING LUSTILY, and with good courage. Beware of singing as if you are half-dead or half-asleep; but lift up your voice with strength. Be no more afraid of your voice now, nor more ashamed of its being heard, than when you sing the songs of Satan.

SING MODESTLY. Do not bawl, so as to be heard above or distinct from the rest of the congregation—that you may not destroy the harmony—but strive to unite your voices together so as to make one clear melodious sound.

SING IN TIME. Whatever time is sung be sure to keep with it. Do not run before nor stay behind it; but attend close to the leading voices, and move therewith as exactly as you can; and take care not to sing *too slow*. This drawling way naturally steals on all who are lazy; and it is high time to drive it out from among us, and sing all our tunes as quick as we did at first.

ABOVE ALL, SING SPIRITUALLY. Have an eye to God in every word you sing. Aim at pleasing him more than yourself, or any other creature. In order to do this, attend strictly to the sense of what you sing, and see that your heart is not carried away with the sound, but offered to God continually; so shall your singing be such as the Lord will approve of here, and reward you when he cometh in the clouds of heaven.

John Wesley, "Directions for Singing"

61   I Will Sing the Wondrous Story

Francis H. Rowley, 1854-1952

WONDROUS STORY 8.7.8.7. *with Refrain*
Peter P. Bilhorn, 1865-1936

1 I will sing the won-drous sto - ry Of the Christ who died for me,
2 I was lost, but Je - sus found me, Found the sheep that went a - stray,
3 I was bruised, but Je - sus healed me, Faint was I from man-y a fall;
4 Days of dark-ness still come o'er me, Sor-row's paths I oft - en tread,

How he left his home in glo - ry For the cross of Cal - va - ry.
Threw his lov - ing arms a - round me, Drew me back in - to the way.
Sight was gone, and fears pos-sessed me, But he freed me from them all.
But the Sav - ior still is with me, By his hand I'm safe - ly led.

REFRAIN

Yes, I'll sing_____ the won-drous sto - ry Of the
Yes, I'll sing the won-drous sto-ry

Christ_____ who died for me, _____ Sing it with_____ the saints in
Of the Christ who died for me, Sing it with

glo - ry, Gath-ered by the crys-tal sea.
the saints in glo-ry, Gath-ered by the crys-tal sea.

Lord, Speak to Me

62

Frances Ridley Havergal, 1836-1879

CANONBURY L.M.
Robert Schumann, 1810-1856

1 Lord, speak to me, that I may speak In
2 O lead me, Lord, that I may lead The
3 O teach me, Lord, that I may teach The
4 O fill me with thy full - ness, Lord, Un -
5 O use me, Lord, use e - ven me, Just

liv - ing ech - oes of thy tone; As thou hast sought, so
wan-d'ring and the wa - v'ring feet; O feed me, Lord, that
pre - cious things thou dost im - part; And wing my words, that
til my ver - y heart o'er-flow In kin - dling thought and
as thou wilt, and when, and where, Un - til thy bless - ed

let me seek Thy err - ing chil - dren lost and lone.
I may feed Thy hun - g'ring ones with man - na sweet.
they may reach The hid - den depths of man - y a heart.
glow-ing word, Thy love to tell, thy praise to show.
face I see— Thy rest, thy joy, thy glo - ry share. A - men.

63 Blessed Assurance, Jesus Is Mine!

Fanny J. Crosby, 1820-1915

ASSURANCE 9.10.9.9. *with Refrain*
Phoebe P. Knapp, 1839-1908

1 Bless-ed as - sur-ance, Je - sus is mine! O what a fore - taste of
2 Per-fect sub - mis-sion, per-fect de - light, Vi-sions of rap - ture now
3 Per-fect sub - mis-sion, all is at rest, I in my Sav - ior am

glo - ry di - vine! Heir of sal - va - tion, pur-chase of God,
burst on my sight; An - gels de - scend-ing bring from a - bove,
hap - py and blest; Watch-ing and wait - ing, look-ing a - bove,

REFRAIN

Born of his Spir - it, washed in his blood.
Ech-oes of mer - cy, whis-pers of love. This is my sto-ry, this is my
Filled with his good-ness, lost in his love.

song, Prais-ing my Sav - ior all the day long; This is my sto - ry,

this is my song, Prais-ing my Sav - ior all the day long.

Like a River Glorious

Frances Ridley Havergal, 1836-1879

64

WYE VALLEY 6.5.6.5.D. *with Refrain*
James Mountain, 1844-1933

1 Like a riv - er glo - rious Is God's per-fect peace, O - ver all vic-
2 Hid-den in the hol - low Of his bless-ed hand, Nev - er foe can
3 Ev -'ry joy or tri - al Fall-eth from a - bove, Traced up-on our

to - rious In its bright in - crease; Per-fect, yet it flow - eth Full - er
fol - low, Nev - er trai - tor stand; Not a surge of wor - ry, Not a
di - al By the sun of love; We may trust him ful - ly All for

ev - 'ry day, Per - fect, yet it grow -eth Deep -er all the way.
shade of care, Not a blast of hur - ry Touch the spir-it there.
us to do— They who trust him whol - ly Find him whol-ly true.

REFRAIN

Stayed up - on Je - ho - vah, Hearts are ful - ly blest—

Find - ing, as he prom - ised, Per - fect peace and rest.

65 He Leadeth Me, O Blessed Thought!

Joseph H. Gilmore, 1834-1918

HE LEADETH ME L.M. *with Refrain*
William B. Bradbury, 1816-1868

1 He lead - eth me, O bless-ed thought! O words with heav'n-ly com-fort fraught!
2 Lord, I would clasp thy hand in mine, Nor ev - er mur - mur nor re-pine;
3 And when my task on earth is done, When by thy grace the vic-t'ry's won,

What - e'er I do, where-e'er I be, Still 'tis God's hand that lead - eth me.
Con - tent, what-ev - er lot I see, Since 'tis my God that lead - eth me.
E'en death's cold wave I will not flee, Since God thru Jor - dan lead - eth me.

REFRAIN

He lead-eth me, he lead-eth me, By his own hand he lead-eth me;

His faith-ful fol-l'wer I would be, For by his hand he lead-eth me.

Savior, Like a Shepherd Lead Us

66

From "Hymns for the Young," 1836
Attr. to Dorothy A. Thrupp, 1779-1847

BRADBURY 8.7.8.7.D.
William B. Bradbury, 1816-1868
Harm. by A. Royce Eckhardt, 1937-

1 Sav-ior, like a shep-herd lead us, Much we need thy ten-der care;
2 We are thine, do thou be-friend us, Be the guard-ian of our way;
3 Thou hast prom-ised to re-ceive us, Poor and sin-ful though we be;
4 Ear-ly let us seek thy fa-vor, Ear-ly let us do thy will;

In thy pleas-ant pas-tures feed us, For our use thy folds pre-pare:
Keep thy flock, from sin de-fend us, Seek us when we go a-stray:
Thou hast mer-cy to re-lieve us, Grace to cleanse and pow'r to free:
Bless-ed Lord and on-ly Sav-ior, With thy love our bos-oms fill:

Bless-ed Je-sus, bless-ed Je-sus, Thou hast bought us, thine we are;
Bless-ed Je-sus, bless-ed Je-sus, Hear, O hear us, when we pray;
Bless-ed Je-sus, bless-ed Je-sus, Ear-ly let us turn to thee;
Bless-ed Je-sus, bless-ed Je-sus, Thou hast loved us, love us still;

Bless-ed Je-sus, bless-ed Je-sus, Thou hast bought us, thine we are.
Bless-ed Je-sus, bless-ed Je-sus, Hear, O hear us, when we pray.
Bless-ed Je-sus, bless-ed Je-sus, Ear-ly let us turn to thee.
Bless-ed Je-sus, bless-ed Je-sus, Thou hast loved us, love us still. A-men.

67 Tell Me the Story of Jesus

Fanny J. Crosby, 1820-1915

STORY OF JESUS 8.7.8.7.D. *with Refrain*
John R. Sweney, 1837-1899

1 Tell me the sto - ry of Je - sus, Write on my heart ev - 'ry word;
2 Fast-ing a - lone in the des - ert, Tell of the days that are past,
3 Tell of the cross where they nailed him, Writh-ing in an- guish and pain;

Ref. Tell me the sto - ry of Je - sus, Write on my heart ev - 'ry word;

Fine

Tell me the sto - ry most pre - cious, Sweet-est that ev - er was heard.
How for our sins he was tempt-ed, Yet was tri - um-phant at last.
Tell of the grave where they laid him, Tell how he liv - eth a - gain.

Tell me the sto - ry most pre - cious, Sweet-est that ev - er was heard.

Tell how the an - gels, in cho - rus, Sang as they wel-comed his birth,
Tell of the years of his la - bor, Tell of the sor - row he bore,
Love in that sto - ry so ten - der, Clear - er than ev - er I see:

D.C. for Refrain

"Glo - ry to God in the high - est! Peace and good ti - dings to earth."
He was de-spised and af - flict - ed, Home-less, re-ject - ed, and poor.
Stay, let me weep while you whis - per, Love paid the ran - som for me.

More About Jesus Would I Know   68

Eliza E. Hewitt, 1851-1920

MORE ABOUT JESUS L.M. *with Refrain*
John R. Sweney, 1837-1899

1 More a-bout Je - sus would I know, More of his grace to oth - ers show;
2 More a-bout Je - sus let me learn, More of his ho - ly will dis-cern;
3 More a-bout Je - sus; in his word, Hold-ing com-mun-ion with my Lord;
4 More a-bout Je - sus on his throne, Rich-es in glo - ry all his own;

More of his sav - ing full-ness see, More of his love who died for me.
Spir-it of God, my teach-er be, Show-ing the things of Christ to me.
Hear-ing his voice in ev - 'ry line, Mak-ing each faith-ful say - ing mine.
More of his king-dom's sure in-crease; More of his com-ing, Prince of Peace.

REFRAIN

More, more a - bout Je - sus, More, more a - bout Je - sus;

More of his sav - ing full-ness see, More of his love who died for me.

69 Wonderful Grace of Jesus

Haldor Lillenas, 1885-1951

WONDERFUL GRACE 7.6.7.6.7.6.12. *with Refrain*
Haldor Lillenas, 1885-1951

1 Won - der - ful grace of Je - sus, Great - er than all my sin;
2 Won - der - ful grace of Je - sus, Reach-ing to all the lost,
3 Won - der - ful grace of Je - sus, Reach-ing the most de - filed,

How shall my tongue de - scribe it, Where shall its praise be - gin?
By it I have been par - doned, Saved to the ut - ter - most;
By its trans-form-ing pow - er Mak - ing him God's dear child,

Tak - ing a - way my bur - den, Set - ting my spir - it free,
Chains have been torn a - sun - der, Giv - ing me lib - er - ty,
Pur - chas-ing peace and heav - en For all e - ter - ni - ty —

For the won - der - ful grace of Je - sus reach - es me.
For the won - der - ful grace of Je - sus reach - es me.
And the won - der - ful grace of Je - sus reach - es me.

CHORUS

the match-less grace of Je - sus,

Won-der-ful the match-less grace of Je - sus, Deep-er

70 Under His Wings I Am Safely Abiding

William O. Cushing, 1828-1902

UNDER HIS WINGS 11.10.11.10 *with Refrain*
Ira D. Sankey, 1840-1908

1 Un - der his wings, I am safe - ly a - bid - ing; Tho' the night
2 Un - der his wings, what a ref - uge in sor - row! How the heart
3 Un - der his wings, O what pre-cious en - joy-ment! There will I

deep-ens and tem-pests are wild, Still I can trust him; I
yearn-ing - ly turns to his rest! Oft - en when earth has no
hide till life's tri - als are o'er; Shel-tered, pro - tect - ed, no

know he will keep me; He has re-deemed me, and I am his child.
balm for my heal-ing, There I find com-fort, and there I am blest.
e - vil can harm me; Rest-ing in Je - sus I'm safe ev - er - more.

REFRAIN

Un-der his wings, un-der his wings, Who from his love can sev-er?

Un-der his wings my soul shall a - bide, Safe-ly a-bide for - ev - er.

When Peace, Like a River, Attendeth My Way

Horatio G. Spafford, 1828-1888

IT IS WELL WITH MY SOUL
Irregular with Refrain
Philip P. Bliss, 1836-1876

1 When peace, like a riv - er, at - tend - eth my way, When sor-rows like
2 Though Sa - tan should buf-fet, tho' tri - als should come, Let this blest as-
3 My sin— oh, the bliss of this glo - ri - ous tho't—My sin— not in
4 And, Lord, haste the day when the faith shall be sight, The clouds be rolled

sea - bil-lows roll; What - ev - er my lot, Thou hast taught me to say,
sur-ance con - trol, That Christ has re - gard - ed my help-less es - tate,
part, but the whole, Is nailed to the cross, and I bear it no more,
back as a scroll, The trum-pet shall sound, and the Lord shall de-scend,

REFRAIN

It is well, it is well with my soul. It is well with my
And hath shed his own blood for my soul.
Praise the Lord, praise the Lord, O my soul! it is well
"E - ven so"— it is well with my soul.

soul, It is well, it is well with my soul.
with my soul,

72   In Shady, Green Pastures

G. A. Young, 19th century

GOD LEADS US
11.8.11.8. *with Refrain*
G. A. Young, 19th century

1 In   shad - y, green pas - tures, so   rich and so sweet, God
2 Some - times on the mount where the   sun shines so bright, God
3 Tho'   sor - rows be - fall   us, and   Sa - tan op - pose, God
4 A -   way from the mire, and a -   way from the clay, God

leads his dear chil-dren a - long;   Where the   wa - ter's cold flow bathes the
leads his dear chil-dren a - long;   Some -   times in the val - ley, in
leads his dear chil-dren a - long;   Through   grace we can con - quer de-
leads his dear chil-dren a - long;   To   walk in the path of the

wea - ry one's feet, God   leads his dear chil - dren a - long.
dark - est of night, God   leads his dear chil - dren a - long.
feat all our foes, God   leads his dear chil - dren a - long.
just ev - ery day, God   leads his dear chil - dren a - long.

REFRAIN

Some thru the wa - ters,   some thru the flood,   Some thru the fire, but

Copyright 1903, by G. A. Young. Renewal 1931. Nazarene Publishing House, owner.

all thru the blood; Some thru great sor - row, but

God gives a song, In the night sea - son and all the day long.

Amazing Grace! How Sweet the Sound 73

John Newton, 1725-1807
John P. Rees, c. 1859-?, St. 5

AMAZING GRACE C.M.
American Melody
Carrell and Clayton's "Virginia Harmony," 1831
Harm. by Edwin O. Excell, 1851-1921

1 A - maz - ing grace! how sweet the sound—That saved a wretch like me!
2 'Twas grace that taught my heart to fear, And grace my fears re - lieved;
3 The Lord has prom - ised good to me, His word my hope se - cures;
4 Thru man - y dan - gers, toils, and snares, I have al - read - y come;
5 When we've been there ten thou - sand years, Bright shin - ing as the sun,

I once was lost but now am found, Was blind but now I see.
How pre - cious did that grace ap - pear The hour I first be - lieved.
He will my shield and por - tion be As long as life en - dures.
'Tis grace hath brought me safe thus far, And grace will lead me home.
We've no less days to sing God's praise Than when we'd first be - gun.

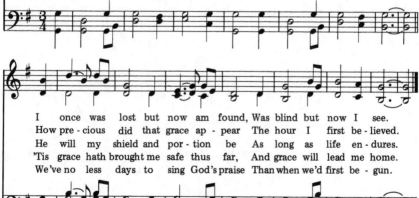

74 My Faith Has Found a Resting Place

Lidie H. Edmunds, 19th century, alt.

NO OTHER PLEA C.M. *with Refrain*
Norwegian Melody

1 My faith has found a rest-ing place, Not in a man-made creed;
2 E - nough for me that Je - sus saves, This ends my fear and doubt;
3 My soul is rest - ing on the Word, The liv - ing Word of God:
4 The great Phy - si - cian heals the sick, The lost he came to save;

I trust the ev - er - liv - ing One, That he for me will plead.
A sin - ful soul I come to him, He will not cast me out.
Sal - va - tion in my Sav - ior's name, Sal - va-tion through his blood.
For me his pre - cious blood he shed, For me his life he gave.

REFRAIN

I need no oth - er ev - i - dence, I need no oth - er plea;

It is e - nough that Je - sus died And rose a - gain for me.

What a Friend We Have in Jesus 75

Joseph Scriven, 1820-1886

ERIE 8.7.8.7.D.
Charles C. Converse, 1832-1918

1 What a friend we have in Je - sus, All our sins and griefs to bear!
2 Have we tri - als and temp - ta - tions? Is there trou-ble an - y-where?
3 Are we weak and heav-y - la - den, Cum-bered with a load of care?

What a priv - i - lege to car - ry Ev - 'ry-thing to God in prayer!
We should nev-er be dis - cour - aged— Take it to the Lord in prayer!
Pre - cious Sav-ior, still our ref - uge— Take it to the Lord in prayer!

O what peace we oft - en for - feit, O what need-less pain we bear,
Can we find a friend so faith - ful, Who will all our sor-rows share?
Do thy friends de-spise, for - sake thee? Take it to the Lord in prayer!

All be-cause we do not car - ry Ev - 'ry-thing to God in prayer.
Je - sus knows our ev - 'ry weak - ness— Take it to the Lord in prayer!
In his arms he'll take and shield thee— Thou wilt find a sol - ace there.

76 Standing on the Promises of Christ

R. Kelso Carter, 1849-1928

PROMISES Irregular *with Refrain*
R. Kelso Carter, 1849-1928

1 Stand-ing on the prom-is-es of Christ my King,
2 Stand-ing on the prom-is-es that can-not fail,
3 Stand-ing on the prom-is-es of Christ the Lord,
4 Stand-ing on the prom-is-es I can-not fall,

Thro' e-ter-nal a-ges let his prais-es ring;
When the howl-ing storms of doubt and fear as-sail,
Bound to him e-ter-nal-ly by love's strong cord,
List-'ning ev-'ry mo-ment to the Spir-it's call,

Glo-ry in the high-est, I will shout and sing,
By the liv-ing Word of God I shall pre-vail,
O-ver-com-ing dai-ly with the Spir-it's sword,
Rest-ing in my Sav-ior, as my all in all,

REFRAIN

Stand-ing on the prom-is-es of God.
Stand-ing on the prom-is-es of God.
Stand-ing on the prom-is-es of God.
Stand-ing on the prom-is-es of God.

Stand-ing, stand-ing,

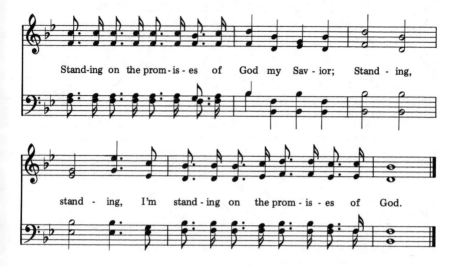

Stand-ing on the prom-is-es of God my Sav-ior; Stand - ing,

stand - ing, I'm stand - ing on the prom - is - es of God.

I will sing with the spirit, and I will sing with the understanding also.

1 Corinthians 14:15 (AV)

Sing so as to make the world hear. The highest value of our singing after all has not been the mere gladness we have felt because of our salvation, but the joy of pouring out the praises of our God to those who have not known him, or of arousing them by our singing to new thoughts and a new life.

And sing till your whole soul is lifted up to God, and then sing till you lift the eyes of those who know not God to him who is the foundation of all our joy!

General William Booth

77   We Have Heard the Joyful Sound

Priscilla J. Owens, 1829-1907

JESUS SAVES 7.3.7.3.7.7.7.3.
William J. Kirkpatrick, 1838-1921

1 We have heard the joy-ful sound: Je-sus saves! Je-sus saves!
2 Waft it on the roll-ing tide: Je-sus saves! Je-sus saves!
3 Sing a-bove the bat-tle strife: Je-sus saves! Je-sus saves!
4 Give the winds a might-y voice: Je-sus saves! Je-sus saves!

Spread the ti-dings all a-round: Je-sus saves! Je-sus saves!
Tell to sin-ners far and wide: Je-sus saves! Je-sus saves!
By his death and end-less life: Je-sus saves! Je-sus saves!
Let the na-tions now re-joice: Je-sus saves! Je-sus saves!

Bear the news to ev-'ry land, Climb the steeps and cross the waves;
Sing, ye is-lands of the sea! Ech-o back, ye o-cean caves!
Sing it soft-ly thru the gloom, When the heart for mer-cy craves;
Shout sal-va-tion full and free, High-est hills and deep-est caves;

On-ward! 'tis our Lord's com-mand: Je-sus saves! Je-sus saves!
Earth shall keep her ju-bi-lee: Je-sus saves! Je-sus saves!
Sing in tri-umph o'er the tomb: Je-sus saves! Je-sus saves!
This our song of vic-to-ry: Je-sus saves! Je-sus saves!

Come to the Savior, Make No Delay 78

George Frederick Root, 1820-1895

COME TO THE SAVIOR
9.9.9.6. *with Refrain*
George Frederick Root, 1820-1895

1 Come to the Sav-ior, make no de-lay; Here in his word he's shown us the way;
2 "Suf - fer the chil-dren!" O hear his voice, Let ev - 'ry heart leap forth and re-joice,
3 Think once a-gain, he's with us to-day; Heed now his blest com-mands, and o-bey;

Here in our midst he's stand-ing to-day, Ten-der - ly say - ing, "Come!"
And let us free - ly make him our choice; Do not de-lay, but come.
Hear now his ac - cents ten - der - ly say, "Will you, my chil-dren, come?"

REFRAIN

Joy-ful, joy - ful will the meet-ing be, When from sin our hearts are pure and free;

And we shall gath - er, Sav - ior, with thee, In our e - ter - nal home.

79 O Safe to the Rock That Is Higher Than I

William O. Cushing, 1823-1902

HIDING IN THEE
11.11.11.11. *with Refrain*
Ira D. Sankey, 1840-1908

1 O safe to the Rock that is high-er than I, My
2 In the calm of the noon-tide, in sor-row's lone hour, In
3 How oft in the con-flict, when pressed by the foe, I have

soul in its con-flicts and sor-rows would fly; So
times when temp-ta-tion casts o'er me its pow'r; In the
fled to my Ref-uge and breathed out my woe; How

sin-ful, so wea-ry, thine, thine, would I be; Thou
tem-pests of life, on its wide, heav-ing sea, Thou
oft-en, when tri-als like sea-bil-lows roll, Have I

REFRAIN

blest "Rock of A-ges," I'm hid-ing in thee.
blest "Rock of A-ges," I'm hid-ing in thee   Hid-ing in thee,
hid-den in thee, O thou Rock of my soul.

Hid - ing in thee, Thou blest "Rock of A - ges," I'm hid - ing in thee.

My Jesus, I Love Thee 80

William R. Featherston, 1846-1873

GORDON 11.11.11.11.
Adoniram J. Gordon, 1836-1895

1 My Je - sus, I love thee, I know thou art mine; For thee all the
2 I love thee be - cause thou hast first lov - ed me, And pur-chased my
3 I'll love thee in life, I will love thee in death, And praise thee as
4 In man-sions of glo - ry and end - less de - light, I'll ev - er a -

fol - lies of sin I re - sign; My gra - cious Re - deem - er, my
par - don on Cal - va - ry's tree; I love thee for wear - ing the
long as thou lend - est me breath; And say when the death - dew lies
dore thee in heav - en so bright; I'll sing with the glit - ter - ing

Sav - ior art thou: If ev - er I loved thee, my Je - sus, 'tis now.
thorns on thy brow: If ev - er I loved thee, my Je - sus, 'tis now.
cold on my brow: If ev - er I loved thee, my Je - sus, 'tis now.
crown on my brow: If ev - er I loved thee, my Je - sus, 'tis now. A-men.

81 I Know Not Why God's Wondrous Grace

Based on 2 Timothy 1:12b
Daniel W. Whittle, 1840-1901

EL NATHAN C.M. *with Refrain*
James McGranahan, 1840-1907

1 I know not why God's won-drous grace To me he has made known,
2 I know not how this sav-ing faith To me he did im-part,
3 I know not how the Spir-it moves, Con-vinc-ing me of sin,
4 I know not when my Lord may come, At night or noon-day fair,

Nor why, un-wor-thy, Christ in love Re-deemed me for his own.
Nor how be-liev-ing in his word Wrought peace with-in my heart.
Re-veal-ing Je-sus thru the word, Cre-at-ing faith in him.
Nor if I walk the vale with him, Or meet him in the air.

REFRAIN

But "I know whom I have be-liev-ed, and am per-suad-ed that he is

a-ble To keep that which I've com-mit-ted Un-to him a-gainst that day."

Jesus Is All the World to Me

Will L. Thompson, 1847-1909

ELIZABETH 8.6.8.6.8.8.8.3.
Will L. Thompson, 1847-1909

1 Je - sus is all the world to me, My life, my joy, my all;
2 Je - sus is all the world to me, My Friend in tri - als sore;
3 Je - sus is all the world to me, And true to him I'll be;
4 Je - sus is all the world to me, I want no bet - ter friend;

He is my strength from day to day, With - out him I would fall.
I go to him for bless-ings, and he gives them o'er and o'er.
Oh, how could I this Friend de - ny, When he's so true to me?
I trust him now, I'll trust him when Life's fleet-ing days shall end.

When I am sad, to him I go, No oth - er one can
He sends the sun - shine and the rain; He sends the har - vest's
Fol - low - ing him I know I'm right, He watch-es o'er me
Beau - ti - ful life with such a Friend; Beau - ti - ful life that

cheer me so; When I am sad He makes me glad, He's my Friend.
gold - en grain; Sun-shine and rain, har-vest of grain, He's my Friend.
day and night; Fol - low - ing him, by day or night, He's my Friend.
has no end; E - ter - nal life, e - ter - nal joy, He's my Friend.

83 When the Trumpet of the Lord Shall Sound

James M. Black, 1859-1936

TRUMPET OF THE LORD
15.11.15.11. *with Refrain*
James M. Black, 1859-1936

1 When the trum-pet of the Lord shall sound, and the
2 On that bright and cloud-less morn-ing when the
3 Let us la-bor for the Mas-ter from the

time shall be no more, And the morn-ing breaks, e-ter-nal, bright and
dead in Christ shall rise, And the glo-ry of his res-ur-rec-tion
dawn till set-ting sun, Let us talk of all his won-drous love and

fair; When the saved of earth shall gath-er o-ver
share; When his cho-sen ones shall gath-er to their
care; Then when all of life is o-ver, and our

on the oth-er shore, And the roll is called up yon-der, I'll be there.
home be-yond the skies, And the roll is called up yon-der, I'll be there.
work on earth is done, And the roll is called up yon-der, I'll be there.

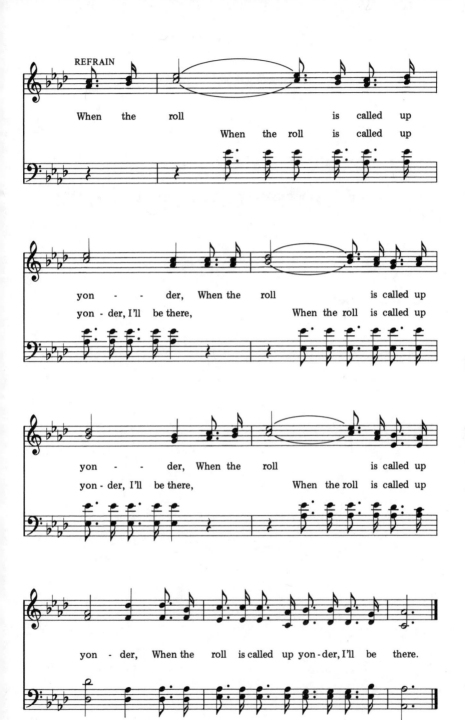

Contemporary Hymns

This Is a Time to Remember

84

Bryan Jeffery Leech, 1931-

DUDLEY 14.14.14.14.
Bryan Jeffery Leech, 1931-
Arr. Roland Tabell, 1934-

1 This is a time to re - mem-ber the great-ness of the Lord.
2 This is a time to re - mem-ber the glo - ries that have been.
3 This is a time to re - mem-ber the church is His, not ours.

He has so faith-ful-ly led us as prom-ised in His Word. ___
This is a time to press on - ward to vis - tas yet un - seen. For
This is a time to sur - ren-der our - selves, our wealth, our pow'rs. ___

He has so boun-ti-f'lly giv - en His grace like fresh-ening rain. ___
Christ is a - live in His peo - ple He meets us face to face. He
This is a time to be ser - vants to give our-selves a - way. ___

He has so lov - ing-ly par-doned and made us whole a - gain.
grants us the pow'r of His Spir - it to serve Him in this place.
Build-ing the church of the fu - ture un - til the com - ing day.

85 Sing Unto the Lord Our King

Dorothy Nordstrom, 1912-

MOLINE 7.5.7.5.7.6.7.5.
Phyllis Nordstrom, 1946-

1 Sing un-to the Lord our King, Praise ho-ly name;
2 Joy is ours through Christ the Son, Born on earth to save,
3 Fu-ture years are in your hands; Help us to re-main

He our con-stant help has been Through all years the same.
Sac-ri-ficed on Cal-va-ry, Ris-en from the grave.
Stead-fast in your ser-vice, Lord, And your Church main-tain.

Thanks be un-to God, we sing, Praise his name for-ev-er.
Thanks be un-to God, we sing, Praise his name for-ev-er.
Thanks be un-to God, we sing, Praise his name for-ev-er.

All his good-ness, love, and grace Joy-ful-ly ac-claim.
Let the mes-sage ev-er ring Of the Son he gave.
Be for-ev-er Lord and King, O-ver us to reign. A-men.

Alleluia No. 1

Don Fishel
Arr. Betty Pulkingham

86

Capo 3 (D)
REFRAIN

Al-le - lu - ia, al-le - lu - ia, give thanks to the ris-en Lord; Al-le-

lu - ia, al-le - lu - ia, give praise to his name.

VERSES

1 Je - sus is Lord of all the earth, He is the
2 Spread the good news o'er all the earth, Je - sus has
3 We have been cru - ci - fied with Christ, Now we shall
4 God has pro - claimed the just re - ward, Life for all
5 Come, let us praise the liv - ing God, Joy - ful - ly

King of cre - a - tion. name.
died and has ris - en.
live for ev - er. Al - le -
peo - ple, al - le - lu - ia.
sing to our Sav - ior.

87 Earth and All Stars

Herbert F. Brokering, 1926-

DEXTER 4.5.7.D. *with Refrain*
David N. Johnson, 1922-
Harm. by Jan Bender, 1909-

In unison

1 Earth and all stars, Loud rush-ing plan - ets,
2 Hail, wind and rain, Loud blow-ing snow - storm,
3 Trum-pet and pipes, Loud clash-ing cym - bals,
4 En - gines and steel, Loud pound-ing ham - mers,
5 Knowl-edge and truth, Loud sound-ing wis - dom,

Sing to the Lord_____ a new song! O vic-to - ry,
Sing to the Lord_____ a new song! Flow-ers and trees,
Sing to the Lord_____ a new song! Harp, lute and lyre,
Sing to the Lord_____ a new song! Lime-stone and beams,
Sing to the Lord_____ a new song! Daugh-ter and son,

Loud shout-ing ar - my, Sing to the Lord_____ a new song!
Loud rus-tling dry leaves, Sing to the Lord_____ a new song!
Loud hum-ming cel - los, Sing to the Lord_____ a new song!
Loud build-ing work-ers, Sing to the Lord_____ a new song!
Loud prais-ing mem-bers, Sing to the Lord_____ a new song!

REFRAIN

He has done mar - vel-ous things: I too will praise him with a new song!

God of Love, You Alone   88
(To Tune of No. 22)

Eric G. Hawkinson, 1896-1984

BEGYNNELSE 12.9.12.9.9.
Wilhelm Theodor Söderberg, 1845-1922
Harm. by James P. Davies, 1913-

God of love, you alone are the fount of our song,
You are worthy to praise and adore.
Lift our hearts unto you, give us joy, make us strong,
Let your Spirit rekindle our faith,
That yours be the glory forever!

O descend as we pray that each heart may be filled
With a joyous and tuneful refrain.
Like the echoes of peace o'er the storm that is stilled
Where the journey is golden again,
And yours be the glory forever!

When our worship is o'er send us forth as of old
To the fields that are already white.
Let the harvest then praise not ourselves but your grace,
In your kingdom's eternal domain,
And yours be the glory forever! Amen.

89   Brothers Come, Sisters Come

Based on Psalms 86:9,10 and 95:6

Dan Whittemore

1 Broth-ers, come;___ sis - ters, come;___ wor - ship Lord Je - sus.___
2 Trav - 'ler, come;___ stran - ger, come;___ wor - ship Lord Je - sus.___
3 Broth-ers, go;___ sis - ters, go;___ wor - ship Lord Je - sus.___
4 Go and live the life he gives:___ wor - ship Lord Je - sus. As

Put a - side all that di - vides; come wor - ship the Lord.
All who fear, you're wel-come here; come wor - ship the Lord.
As we grow, our love will show we wor - ship the Lord.
we de - part, we on - ly start to wor - ship the Lord.

REFRAIN

Sing him prais - es, all his___ peo - ple.

(1,2) Broth-ers, come; sis - ters, come;___ wor - ship the Lord.
(3,4) Broth-ers, go; sis - ters, go; ___

Praise and Thanksgiving

90

Albert F. Bayly, 1901-, alt.

BUNESSAN 5.5.5.4.D.
Gaelic

1. Praise and thanks-giv - ing, Fa - ther, we of - fer For all things liv - ing, Cre - at - ed good: Har-vest of sown fields, Fruits of the or - chard, Hay from the mown fields, Blos-som and wood.
2. Bless, Lord, the la - bor We bring to serve you, That with our neigh - bor We may be fed. Sow-ing or till - ing, We would work with you, Har-vest-ing, mill - ing, For dai - ly bread.
3. Fa - ther, pro - vid - ing Food for your chil - dren, By your wise guid - ing Teach us to share One with an - oth - er, So that, re - joic - ing With us, all oth - ers May know your care.
4. Then will your bless - ing Reach ev - 'ry peo - ple, Free-ly con - fess - ing Your gra-cious hand. Where all o - bey you, No one will hun - ger; In your love's sway you Nour-ish the land.

Anyone possessed of his five wits should blush with shame if he did not begin the day with a psalm, since even the tiniest birds open and close the day with sweet songs of holy devotion.

St. Ambrose

Thou Art Worthy

91

Pauline M. Mills

Thou art wor-thy, Thou art wor-thy, Thou art wor-thy, O Lord,_____ To re-ceive glo-ry,_ glo-ry and hon-or, glo-ry and hon-or and pow'r._____ For thou hast cre-a-ted, hast all things cre-a-ted; Thou hast cre-a-ted all things._____ And for thy pleas-ure

they are cre - a - ted, for thou art wor -thy, O Lord.____

Bless His Holy Name

92

Andraé Crouch, 1945-

BLESS THE LORD
Andraé Crouch, 1945-

Bless the Lord, O my soul, and all that is with - in me bless his

Fine

ho - ly name. He has done great things, He has done great

D.C. al Fine

things, He has done great things, Bless his ho - ly name.

93   O How He Loves You and Me!

Kurt Kaiser, 1934-

HE LOVES YOU AND ME 7.7.9.5.5.7.
Kurt Kaiser, 1934-

1 O how he loves you and me!
2 Je - sus to Cal - v'ry did go,

O how he loves you and me.
His love for us then to show.

He gave his life— what more could he give?
What he did there brought hope from de - spair:

O how he loves you, O how he loves me,
O how he loves you, O how he loves me,

O how he loves you and me.
O how he loves you and me.

We Are One in the Bond of Love 94

Otis Skillings, 1935-

BOND OF LOVE 8.8.6.6.8.
Otis Skillings, 1935-

1 We are one in the bond of love, We are one in the
2 Let us sing now, ev - 'ry - one, Let us feel his

bond of love; We have joined our spir - it with the
love be - gun; Let us join our hands that the

Spir - it of God, We are one in the bond of love.
world will know We are one in the bond of love.

A most interesting sight is offered in the city on the weekdays, when the hour for the sermon approaches. As soon as the first sound of the bell is heard, all shops are closed, all conversation ceases, all business is broken off, and from all sides the people hasten to the nearest meeting house. There each one draws from his pocket a small book which contains the psalms with notes, and out of full hearts, in the native speech, the congregation sings before and after the sermon. Every one testifies to me how great consolation and edification is derived from this custom.

A visitor to Geneva in 1557

95 The City Is Alive, O God

William W. Reid, Jr., 1923-

ALL SAINTS NEW C.M.D.
Henry S. Cutler, 1824-1902

1 The cit-y is a-live, O God, With sound of hus-tling feet,
2 Is it your will, O lov-ing God, That rac-es live in strife?
3 To those in an-cient Gal-i-lee Your serv-ant Christ de-clared
4 O God, in-spire your Church to-day To take Christ's serv-ant role,

With flash-ing lights and rap-id change That pulse thru ev-'ry street;
That lone-li-ness and greed and hate Should mark a cit-y's life?
Thru heal-ing touch, thru word and cross, The good news that he cared;
To love the world, to hear its claims, To sense its yearn-ing soul;

But oft there's in-hu-man-i-ty Be-hind the bright fa-cade,
Do you de-sire the rich one's wealth To keep the poor one poor?
He said your heart touched ev-'ry heart That longed for peace and right,
To live with-in the mar-ket place, To serve both weak and strong,

And emp-ty souls with hun-gry hearts Cry out for help, O God.
Must crimes and slums and lust a-bound? O Lord, is there no cure?
That those bowed down by bur-dens borne Could find your life, your light.
To lose her-self, to share her dream, To give the world her song. A-men.

Words copyright 1969 by The Hymn Society of America,
Texas Christian University, Fort Worth, TX 76129.
Used by permission.

Lift High the Cross

96

George W. Kitchin, 1827-1912
Michael R. Newbolt, 1874-1956, alt.

CRUCIFER 10.10.10.10.
Sydney H. Nicholson, 1875-1947

REFRAIN *(In unison)*

Lift high the cross, the love of Christ pro - claim Till all the world a - dore his sa - cred name.

Fine

In parts

1 Come, Chris - tians, fol - low where our Sav - ior trod,
2 Led on their way by this tri - um - phant sign,
3 O Lord, once lift - ed on the glo - rious tree,
4 So shall our song of tri - umph ev - er be:

D.C. al Fine

As thou hast prom - ised, draw us all to thee.
Praise to the Cru - ci - fied for vic - to - ry!
Our king vic - to - rious, Christ, the Son of God.
The hosts of God in con - qu'ring ranks com - bine.

97 Your Cause Be Mine, Great Lord Divine

Bryan Jeffery Leech, 1931-

RICHMOND BEACH 8.7.8.7.8.8.7.
A. Royce Eckhardt, 1937-

In unison

1 Your cause be mine, great Lord di - vine, Your aim be my am - bi - tion: For wast-ed is my great-est strength Un - less it find ex - pres - sion In love that gives it - self a - way, In life re - spon -

2 Your cause be mine, great Lord di - vine, This be my life's vo - ca - tion: To seek the prize when life is done— Your lov - ing ap - pro - ba - tion. Di - min - ish pride, in - crease my love, O may your Spir -

3 Your cause be mine, great Lord di - vine, The world's e - man - ci - pa - tion: To let your light in - vade the dark In ev - 'ry sit - u - a - tion, To prove you in a thou - sand ways, To serve you well

sive to o - bey   The terms of your com - mis - sion.
it   now re - move All self - ish mo - ti - va - tion.
with zeal a - blaze Thru life's un - known du - ra - tion. A - men.

In My Life, Lord, Be Glorified   98

Bob Kilpatrick   Bob Kilpatrick

1 In   my   life, Lord,   Be glo-ri-fied,   Be glo-ri-fied.
2 In   my   song, Lord,   Be glo-ri-fied,   Be glo-ri-fied.
3 In your church, Lord, Be glo-ri-fied, Be glo-ri-fied.

In   my   life, Lord,   Be glo-ri-fied to - day.
In   my   song, Lord,   Be glo-ri-fied to - day.
In your church, Lord, Be glo-ri-fied to - day.

99

Hope of Tomorrow

Richard Carlson, 1956 -

(Comissioned by Covenant Women)

TACOMA
Richard Carlson, 1956-

1 As the sun - rise is hope for the morn - ing, Ev - er
2 There's a prom - ise to claim if we're wait - ing, For a
3 There is peace for the ones who are wait - ing; There is

ris - ing to start new days. _____ So the hope of a
sun - rise with - in our souls. _____ Je - sus of - fers him-
joy for the qui - et soul. _____ There's a treas - ure for

heart that is bro - ken Is the one who is
self as our por - tion; He's the strong - hold in
those who are seek - ing Af - ter Je - sus, the

REFRAIN

faith - ful in grace. _____ Je - sus is
which we have hope! _____ Je - sus is
au - thor of hope. _____

faith - ful, _____ (faith - ful,) Ev - er the

same, (the same). Hope _____ of to - mor - row, Praise his name!_____

Following the example of the prophets and fathers of the Church, I intend to make German psalms for the people, i.e., spiritual songs, so that the Word of God even by means of song may live among the people.

I give music the highest and most honorable place; and everyone knows how David and all the saints put their divine thoughts into verse, rhyme, and song.

I am not of the opinion that all sciences should be beaten down and made to cease by the Gospel, as some fanatics pretend, but I would fain see all the arts, and music in particular, used in the service of him who hath given and created them.

If any man despises music, as all fanatics do, for him I have no liking; for music is a gift and grace of God, not an invention of men. Thus it drives out the devil and make people cheerful. Then one forgets all wrath, impurity, sycophancy, and other vices.

Martin Luther

The hymnbook reflects the history of the Church, embodies the doctrine of the Church, expresses the devotional feeling of the Church, and demonstrates the unity of the Church.

W.M. Taylor

100 Stand Up and Praise the Lord Your God

Susan J. Kinsman, 1963-

FARMHILL 8.5.8.6.8.6.8.6.
Jonathan Brown, 1951-

1 Stand up and praise the Lord your God, Bless his glo-rious name, Whose
2 Stand up and thank the Lord your God, Praise his name a - gain, The
3 Stand up and serve the Lord your God, Let his praise be heard, En-

Cov - e - nant with us has been Through-out all years the same.
one de - serv - ing of our praise Whose love will nev - er end.
trust - ed to us is the charge To live and share his Word.

He saved us thru his on - ly Son, We're chil-dren by his grace; Con-
Though moun-tains may be bro-ken down And all the hills re - moved, His
We earn - est - ly ac - cept the call, De - ny - ing self for him; En-

firmed we raise our joy - ful song His good-ness to pro - claim.
cov - e - nant and stead-fast love For us will still re - main.
a - bled by the Spir - it's pow'r We're made a - live to serve.

INDEX OF FIRST LINES AND TITLES

49 A Mighty Fortress Is Our God
42 All Hail the Power of Jesus' Name
86 Alleluia, Alleluia, Give Thanks
86 Alleluia No. 1
44 Alleluia! Sing to Jesus!
73 Amazing Grace! How Sweet the Sound
38 And Can It Be That I Should Gain
99 As the Sunrise Is Hope for the Morning
52 Be Thou My Vision
43 Beautiful Savior! King of Creation!
92 Bless His Holy Name
92 Bless the Lord, O My Soul
63 Blessed Assurance, Jesus Is Mine!
89 Brothers Come, Sisters Come
19 Children of the Heavenly Father
7 Chosen Seed and Zion's Children
40 Come, Christians, Join to Sing
10 Come, Let Us Praise Him
57 Come, Thou Fount of Every Blessing
78 Come to the Savior, Make No Delay
59 Come, We That Love the Lord
41 Crown Him with Many Crowns
18 Day by Day, and with Each Passing Moment
87 Earth and All Stars
56 For All the Saints
47 God of Grace and God of Glory
88 God of Love, You Alone
23 Great Hills May Tremble
50 Great Is Thy Faithfulness
65 He Leadeth Me, O Blessed Thought!
36 Holy, Holy, Holy! Lord God Almighty!
99 Hope of Tomorrow
48 How Firm a Foundation
5 How Great the Joy the Lord Provides
27 How Wonderful It Is
14 I Have a Friend Who Loveth Me
21 I Have a Future All Sublime
81 I Know Not Why God's Wondrous Grace
17 I Sing of the Savior
11 I Sing with Joy and Gladness
61 I Will Sing the Wondrous Story
22 I with Thee Would Begin
35 Immortal, Invisible, God Only Wise
98 In My Life, Lord, Be Glorified
72 In Shady, Green Pastures
25 In the Springtime Fair
8 In Thy Temple Courts, O Father
82 Jesus Is All the World to Me
6 Jesus, Jesus, Name Most Precious
53 Lead On, O King Eternal
96 Lift High the Cross

64 Like a River Glorious
62 Lord, Speak to Me
68 More About Jesus Would I Know
74 My Faith Has Found a Resting Place
12 My God, When I Consider
54 My Hope Is Built on Nothing Less
80 My Jesus, I Love Thee
26 My Soul Now Magnifies the Lord
31 Now Thank We All Our God
39 O for a Thousand Tongues to Sing
37 O God, Our Help in Ages Past
29 O How Blest to Be a Pilgrim
93 O How He Loves You and Me!
 9 O Let Your Soul Now Be Filled with Gladness
51 O Master, Let Me Walk with Thee
 2 O Mighty God, When I Behold the Wonder
79 O Safe to the Rock That Is Higher Than I
33 O Worship the King All Glorious Above
 3 Our Mighty God Works Mighty Wonders
90 Praise and Thanksgiving
58 Praise Him! Praise Him!
34 Praise, My Soul, the King of Heaven
 1 Praise the Lord, All Praise and Blessing
 4 Praise the Lord with Joyful Song
32 Praise to the Lord, the Almighty
66 Savior, Like a Shepherd Lead Us
45 Sing Hallelujah, Praise the Lord!
85 Sing Unto the Lord, Our King
100 Stand Up and Praise the Lord Your God
76 Standing on the Promises of Christ
67 Tell Me the Story of Jesus
13 Thanks to God for My Redeemer
55 The Church's One Foundation
95 The City Is Alive, O God
15 The Highest Joy That Can Be Known
84 This Is a Time to Remember
91 Thou Art Worthy
24 Thy Holy Wings, Dear Savior
60 To God Be the Glory
70 Under His Wings I Am Safely Abiding
94 We Are One in the Bond of Love
46 We Come, O Christ, to Thee
77 We Have Heard the Joyful Sound
30 We Wait for a Great and Glorious Day
75 What a Friend We Have in Jesus
16 When My Lord Is Dear to Me
71 When Peace, Like a River, Attendeth My Way
83 When the Trumpet of the Lord Shall Sound
28 Why Should I Be Anxious?
20 With God as Our Friend
69 Wonderful Grace of Jesus
97 Your Cause Be Mine, Great Lord Divine